GROW REGARDLESS

"*Grow Regardless* is practical and compelling. It is a must read for every business leader trying to compete in this ever-changing financial world. *Grow Regardless* defines our purpose."

—**Bob Compton**, CFO, Agora Publishing

"Knowing Joe Mechlinski for a number of years and having had the opportunity to work with him, I share my passion for what Joe is addressing in *Grow Regardless*. He is taking a refreshing approach that is so needed during this time of uncertainty. This book is an excellent resource for anyone involved in a small business. It is especially timely in our current challenging economic conditions, and the ideas and guidance are relevant for the better times to come as well. Mechlinski begs the reader to understand the why that is necessary to grow regardless. And understanding why an organization wants to grow is the first true step in growing regardless. His book is a must read."

—**Kathy Albarado**, CEO, Helios HR

"Grow Regardless, provides a unique perspective combining both bottom line numbers with overhauling your culture resulting in a practical guide to revolutionize your organization."

—**Connor Marsden**, US Director of CRM, Microsoft

"Joe Mechlinski has written an indispensable how-to guide for every small-to-medium-sized business leader in America who wants to grow despite all the odds stacked against them."

—**Doug Beigel**, CEO, COLA

"There are many books about, and many voices opining on, business development. Joe's Grow Regardless is not one to miss. Straight-on yet surprisingly, it's a mas-up of 'how-to' and 'inspirational'."

—**Ned Johnson**, President, Prep Matters

"*Grow Regardless* lays out a practical approach for shaking up your business to achieve real breakthroughs in performance. I'm a believer in this approach - through its application we have a clearer vision and mission and most importantly, a compelling story that everyone OWNs. The impact on our employees has been remarkable. As a company who practices change management, I've found the approach and energy of *Grow Regardless* to be a great framework for making the complex and challenging aspects of change simple and solvable."

—**Sue Evans**, President and CEO, Evans Incorporated

"Inspiring, insightful and invaluable lessons for crushing the obstacles and achieving success."

—**Amy Pearl**, President, RV Rhodes LLC

"Chock full of personal anecdotes and real world examples, *Grow Regardless* feels more like advice from your best friend than a "how-to" from an expert consultant. Joe Mechlinski offers a revolutionary approach to sales that will have every business leader asking themself if it's time to hit the RESET button."

—**Chris Gaito**, Partner,
Institutional Sales Furey Research Partners

"Having hired Joe and entreQuest in three of my prior businesses, I know first-hand the dramatic and positive impact his methods have on an organizations. He's a true visionary and leader in business management and has taught me how my organizations can 'grow regardless'."

—**Len Ostroff**, CEO, Authntk, Inc.

"For over a decade, I have witnessed Joe Mechlinski live the principles set forth in Grow Regardless. This book has clarified and simplified the fundamental methods that have contributed to much of my success in business and coaching. Grow Regardless applies to sports teams, as well as business. If you want to transform a losing team into a winning team, it is critical to employ these strategies. I am forever grateful for this wisdom and excited for every reader's future success."

—**Harrison Bernstein**, Owner & CEO,
Satori Sports, LLC and football coach

"It's easy to complain about the bad economy, painful regulations, tough competitors, unproductive employees and difficult customers. It's easy to find reasons why your business can't grow. But Joe can show you how to build your business in spite of these negative factors. If you want to get bigger, if you want to get better, if you want to move past all the excuses, this encouraging and practical book will give you hope and a plan."

—**David Rendall**, CEO, Rendall & Associates and author of
The Freak Factor and *The Four Factors of Effective Leadership*

"If every entrepreneur in America followed Mechlinski's simple growth method, there would be nothing stopping us."

—**John Walden**, President, VibrAlign, Inc.

"Joe is living proof that when energy meets mission growth happens. Grow Regardless is his recipe for the scrappy, smart, sensible and sensitive secret sauce of success. A must read for anybody who wants to jump start, kick start or start over."

—**Greg Conderacci**, President and Founder,
Good Ground Consulting LLC

"I have learned from personal experience how to practice the concept of starting my day over any time I choose, also I recognize that each day is the first day of the rest of my life. This helps me relate to and believe in what Joe is saying with the word and concept RESET. In order for me to RESET, there must be a form of surrender on my part. I often refer to it as Surrender to win!"

—**Stan Stokes**, President, K.C. Company, Inc.

"They say a goal without a plan is just a wish… so many business people spend so much time working in their business that they aren't working 'on it'. *Grow Regardless* will not just help identify the distance between where you are and where you want to be but help with the critical 'travel' step. How do we get there? Think of it as your business' flight plan. Great read Joe!"

—**Larry Cain**, Managing Partner, 3 Dogs Marketing, LLC

"*Grow Regardless* fills a much-needed gap in the business literature and will be a welcome read to any individual with an interest in the realities of running and growing a business. Filled with insights that trigger innumerable "aha moments" (as well as the occasional "oh crap, I need to do that better"), Joe's wisdom, frameworks and processes will provide immense value to leaders of businesses large and small, successful and struggling, established and start-up. By providing a compelling framework, sound support for his principles, specific, hands-on steps with real-life examples delivered in a wonderfully conversational tone, *Grow Regardless* is a joy to read and has earned it the top-spot on my 'books to recommend to clients and friends' list. Having personally had an opportunity to work with Joe, I can honestly say that the only thing that would make it better is if it came with an opportunity to sit down with Joe and experience his enthusiasm and insights first-hand. Until that opportunity arises, *Grow Regardless* will have to do. The good news is that it will do quite well. This is a book that you do not want to miss."

—**David Hyatt**, President and Founder, ON, Inc.

"I had the opportunity to work with Joe and the entreQuest team as they supported our firm with management team building and strategic planning. Although this book was not available at the time, I see many of the successful techniques used in our sessions incorporated in this book. I am sure that any organization can benefit from reading and adapting this approach within their organization."

—**Barry Goldin**, Vice President, Audio Video Systems, Inc.

"Mechlinski offers a wide range of applications for business, community life, and personal development. *Grow Regardless* is a must-have for any business leader looking to build and thrive from positive company culture."

—**Chris Krause**, Founder and CEO, National Collegiate Scouting Association

"*Grow Regardless* is an amazing book that has motivated me to more closely align my personal vision and purpose with my business. This simple methodology is allowing me to create a stronger road map to grow my business to levels I have not previously achieved after 15 years of owning my own company. I was attracted to Mechlinski's mission driven growth methodology as it aligns closely with my personal desire to always give back and grow. In honoring clients, employees and the community with empathy, honesty, and transparency we can grow based on the strength of our relationships; shielded from outside obstacles. The book outlines simple methods for increasing revenues regardless of business challenges and this should be attractive to all business owners focused on the future; especially in today's uncertain economic climate."

—**Christine L. Delucchi**, President & CEO,
Delucchi + and Blue Bug Digital

"This book is a treasure. In a very understandable and clear way, Joe reveals a foundational path to true growth, regardless... He helps you understand the essential, but often overlooked, linkages between emotional intelligence, your own personal "why's" and a "remarkable experience" mindset toward external and internal customers. His sincerity and authenticity are refreshing."

—**David Powell**, COO, Federal Business Council, Inc.

"If you're a business leader who is determined to grow your organization even in troubled economic times, *Grow Regardless* is your blueprint for success."

—**David Zdrojewski**, CEO, VibrAlign, Inc.

"The ideas outlined in Mechlinski's methodology are the necessary building blocks of any growth organization. They create the sustainable foundation necessary before the tactics and execution of a growth plan should be implemented. We have seen an immediate impact in our company's mindset and culture. A true winning formula!"

—**Doug Horensky**, President, Varia Systems, Inc.

"Joe Mechlinski's new book is a must read, must incorporate, must integrate into your corporate culture manifesto.

The only way to get ahead of technology and globalization is to hit RESET, an important theme in Joe's book. As a digital media company that is trying to survive by resetting on a real time basis, Joe's new book is a roadmap for managing in these exciting, dynamic and challenging times where disruption is the norm. Go read "Grow Regardless..." regardless.

—**Edwin Warfield**, CEO, citybizList

"I was introduced to Joe and the entreQuest team 8 years ago. I've listened, learned, and even attended entreQuest training events. His entrepreneurial spirit is admirable and infectious, so much so, that I left my job with a Fortune 500 company and soon began my own business. We follow the "grow regardless" mentality and it's been the key to our business success."

—**Ron Bratz**, President, LiftOff LLC

"Mechlinski and the entreQuest team deployed this methodology first-hand within my organization. In the last 12 months we have enjoyed 100% at margins exceeding our budgetary targets."

—**Neal Lawson**, President, Intelligent Discovery Solutions, Inc.

"Not only proven, but a refreshingly engaging and powerful approach. Few of today's business books go beyond the promise of shortcuts to success; Joe's stands out, digging at the roots, to create lasting value for business owners. Joe's more than an author, I know him as a doer - a business builder that never settles."

—**Matt Schubert**, Former CEO, Social Solutions

"We challenged entreQuest to identify and find sales talent for a dynamic asphalt paving firm. The hiring process was thorough, resulting in four new salespersons hired. Five years on with 100% intervening growth, all four estimators are still employed and highly valued asset to our business."

—**Harold C. Green**, CEO, Chamberlain Contractors, Inc.

"We hired Joe to evaluate our firm from top to bottom and make recommendations to ensure our growing, entrepreneurial firm was on the right track. Joe and his team were extremely professional, thought provoking, straight shooters and offered real world, business solutions which could actually be implemented. They presented their findings in a digestible form and recommended action steps which were extremely helpful. They addressed all components of our business that are vital to our growth and success from our corporate strategy and organization, management, employees and clients. This book shares those philosophies, methodologies and strategies and is a must read for any business owner or manager looking to lead a better company."

—**Jason Hanges**, Managing Partner, Quest Group

"Joe Mechlinski's book, *Grow Regardless* is both substantively and symbolically important for the nation's small business community. In the case of the latter, virtually all the 'business bibles' draw on the experience of huge companies and are written by academics or consultants who rarely have experience in the trenches of small business. This is definitely not the case with Joe's work and he deserves special thanks from small business owners for sharing his wisdom and specific recommendations that they can actually apply.

His encouragement that even the smallest of business can—and in fact —must think, plan, and act beyond the day's constraints to truly succeed is dead on and an especially important message for small business owners. Joe understands that profit is always a byproduct of bringing value to ones employee's, ones customer's and ones relationships. He and his company, entreQuest walk their talk and his recommendations ring true."

—**Roger Ralph**, Co-Founder,
Bel Air Athletic Club & Hockessin Athletic Club

"Joe Mechlinski offers us the kind of commonsense- but not common practice - advice that needs to be at the heart of every company's growth strategy. Purposeful, provocative, and poignant, this book leads you onto the launching pad for true success. Speaking of heart, Joe writes - and lives and works - with a compelling combination of smart, sharp thinking, as well as deep, meaningful feeling. This is a treasure chest of possibilities and practices for everyone who is committed to real growth and success."

—**Steve Lishansky**, CEO, Optimize International

"Joe Mechlinski has a gift for understanding the basis from which to build and grow a successful business. Growing is not a dream, but a "mindset" that Joe spells out for anyone to understand. He also provides a clear road map to follow to achievement. Joe's principles enlighten myself and my employees to an "AhHa" moment from which growth took us to the next level of success."

—**Marylou Goehrung**, President,
Hunt Graphics, Inc. d/b/a Signs By Tomorrow

"For those looking to build their business and take it to the next level regardless of the external challenges in their marketplace or industry, this is a must read. Everyone needs a mentor; someone who tells it like it is and shows you a new way to think about how to lead our teams. Joe is that person. If you want to create an extraordinary business or are wondering how to get to the next level, this is the road map you have been seeking ,but never knew you were missing-until now!"

—**Richard Silberstein**, President, Silberstein Insurance Group

GROW
REGARDLESS

Of Your Business' Size,
Your Industry or the Economy...
and Despite the Government!

JOE MECHLINSKI

NEW YORK

GROW REGARDLESS

Of Your Business' Size, Your Industry or the Economy…and Despite the Government!

ISBN 978-1-61448-435-6 paperback
ISBN 978-1-61448-436-3 eBook
Library of Congress Control Number: 2012954097

Morgan James Publishing
The Entrepreneurial Publisher
5 Penn Plaza, 23rd Floor
New York City, New York 10001
(212) 655-5470 office • (516) 908-4496 fax
www.MorganJamesPublishing.com

Cover Design by:
Rachel Lopez
www.r2cdesign.com

Interior Design by:
Bonnie Bushman
bonnie@caboodlegraphics.com

In an effort to support local communities, raise awareness and funds, Morgan James Publishing donates a percentage of all book sales for the life of each book to Habitat for Humanity Peninsula and Greater Williamsburg.

Get involved today, visit
www.MorganJamesBuilds.com.

This book is dedicated to my mom, my dad and Rose, the three best parents I could have asked for, who taught me to always grow regardless.

TABLE OF CONTENTS

It is not the critic who counts, not the man who points out how the strong man stumbled, or when the doer of deeds could have done better. The credit belongs to the man who is actually in the arena; whose face is marred by dust and sweat and blood; who strives valiantly; who errs and comes short again and again; who knows the great enthusiasms, the great devotions and spends himself in a worthy cause; who at the best, knows in the end the triumph of high achievement; and who at the worst if he fails, at least fails while daring greatly, so that his place shall never be with those cold and timid souls who know neither victory nor defeat.

—Theodore Roosevelt

Foreword

I'VE READ A LOT of books about business over the years. As a broad generalization, they fall into two categories: those based on objective study of data (think *Good to Great*) and those based on more subjective interpretations of personal experience (say, *Think and Grow Rich*).

Data-based books offer the comfort of assurance that "this is how things are," but can leave the reader wondering what to actually do to activate the insights. Alternatively, the firsthand books make it clear what the author did, but leave readers not at all confident they will have the same experience.

I mention this because *Grow Regardless* inhabits an unusual middle ground. While Joe Mechlinski has clearly written a book based on his own experiences, the model he has developed and the power of his conclusions are quite remarkable. The result is a book that not only conveys Mechlinski's considerable passion, but leaves you knowing, without a doubt, that he has got it basically, fundamentally, and deeply right.

Can You Really Grow Regardless?

Mechlinski confronts head-on the notion that people, or businesses, are inherently limited by their size, their industry, the economy, interest rates, and so on. He's hardly the only inspirational author to argue that, in light of said limitations, dreams can come true.

But Mechlinski goes further. He explains how better performance is not simply gotten at the expense of others, or available only to a privileged few. Seriously better performance is available to everyone, including at the industry or economy level. And as you read his prescriptions, you realize he is quite right. This book is not about gaining market share; it's entirely about creating real economic value—regardless of your situation.

Credibility

When I first met Mechlinski, I was impressed by his energy, his graciousness, and his clear commitment to excellence. What I didn't know was how he had gotten there; his personal story is one of great achievement against significant odds. As a youth, he was disadvantaged and devalued at every turn—a real underdog if there ever was one.

Throughout it all, he continued to learn from others. But one of the most important lessons Mechlinski learned was one he learned on his own: to be guided by a small number of core ideas and values. Mechlinski has built a thriving consulting practice founded on those core ideas and values. He works with his client organizations to build businesses based on those same ideas and values. The success of his own consulting business—and it is objectively quite successful, in the top ten percent of his line of business—is a testimony to his ideas. More importantly, so are the stories of the five leaders, clients of his, profiled in his book, who have not only taken on these beliefs as their own, but also directly helped to refine his ideas and philosophies.

Reading these stories, I had the repeated sensation of thinking, "Well, yes, that is how things work, isn't it?" That's the same feeling I have when reading data-based books. But I also had the sensation of thinking, "That is exactly how you do it, isn't it?" And that's the feeling I get from subjective, first-person books.

The Program

Plenty of books will tell you that business is mainly about relationships. Jim Heskett, whom Mechlinski cites, wrote years ago about the important link between great employee relationships and great customer relationships. Dan Pink, as Mechlinski also notes, has written about motivation, and Daniel Goleman about EQ, or the emotional quotient. Mechlinski knows these sources; he's read and absorbed them seriously. But unlike all those dispassionate observers of business success, Mechlinski *feels* these truths. He *lives* these truths. Others have discovered objective data, but Mechlinski has subjectively verified it. He knows that beliefs drive behavior, and so he is quite insistent about the power of beliefs and mindsets.

Mechlinski has uniquely packaged and synthesized these truths into an utterly enjoyable read. **The eQ Growth Methodology™** is deceptively simple: relationships, story, and employees; the three Ps: philosophy, process, and practice; and the five power concepts, including *Hit the Reset Button* and *Start with Why*. Unfortunately, to list them is not to understand them. I did not magically "get" *Grow Regardless* by reading the Table of Contents, and you probably won't either. That's not how human beings work.

So, do yourself the favor of reading this book slowly. Savor it. Then, pass it on to others. That's how it works. And that's how you can make it work for you—and for all the teams, groups and systems of which you are a part.

Charles H. Green
West Orange, NJ
January 23, 2012

INTRODUCTION

Let him that would move the world, first move himself.
—**Socrates**

Why Should We All Care?

We Americans may not agree on much—our opinions are as varied as our diverse population, our politics as divided as the Grand Canyon. But whenever we're faced with a major test of our collective mettle, we somehow manage to pull ourselves together and set aside our differences long enough to get the job done. Whether it was the challenge of putting a man on the moon, ending the Cold War, or eradicating killer diseases, it seems as if there's nothing that American ingenuity, perseverance, optimism, and elbow grease haven't been able to overcome. This is especially true when you take into account the role of small-to-midsize businesses, which increasingly provide the vital lifeblood of our economy.

Even so, in the wake of the recession, I've seen many business leaders suffering from a seeming inability to pick themselves up, shake off the disillusionment, and move forward with a driven determination to achieve new heights, no matter what. Honestly, who can blame us for our negativity?

For years, we've been bombarded with one discouraging business story after another, followed by a never-ending parade of dismal financial statistics, all tied up with a giant red bow of grim economic predictions. Headlines about debt ceilings, credit ratings, and budget plans are commonplace. Families struggle to figure out how to enjoy life to the fullest without racking up credit card debt. Banks are failing. Companies are being shuttered. Unprecedented numbers of workers are losing their jobs and treading the waters of chronic unemployment or underemployment. Gas prices go up, and incomes go down. Wild fluctuations in the global market are giving investors the willies. Governments around the world are fighting to avoid debt defaults, and shutdowns, while other countries jockey to knock us off our perch and become the new twenty-first-century superpowers.

To top it all off, our political leaders are unable to figure out what to do about any of it. It doesn't matter whether we are Democrat or Republican, Libertarian, or Independent, Green Party or Tea Party—more and more of us are beginning to view Washington's problems as our own. Whether you're in favor of tax increases, staunchly anti-tax, or an advocate of something in between, there's no denying that the government today is not our friend. There is probably not a single American who thinks our elected officials are decent role models for us these days. Year after year, they've called upon us to tighten our belts, while being unwilling to make sacrifices of their own. If ordinary people like you and me followed our leaders' examples and went home without doing our jobs more than once or twice, we'd be toast. Not so for the folks in Washington. The double standard is sickening.

Rather than having faith in our leaders to find common ground and take action to stimulate the economy, we sense that they're mostly concerned with self-preservation and with getting re-elected. Many of our political leaders have a short-term focus, and it is squarely on themselves.

What they're doing—or actually, not doing—is the antithesis of leadership. In a nutshell, nobody in Washington wants to take responsibility, and we, the people, are increasingly cynical about our ailing economy and its chances of a full recovery.

But a gridlocked government doesn't have to hold us back, and neither does big business. Contrary to popular belief, small and midsize businesses are the *real* job creators in America. According to the US Bureau of Labor Statistics, companies with fewer than 500 employees created 64 percent of net new jobs from 1992 to 2010.[1] Bloomberg reports that by the spring of 2012, small businesses were creating more jobs than big companies and doing so faster than they had during the 2001 downturn.[2]

In the midst of a hostile business environment, these companies have managed to *grow regardless*. These companies were hiring when others were firing. They were ramping up their strategies while others were closing down operations. They were up-selling their offerings while many large companies were downsizing divisions. Today, after years of doing business in a severe economic slump, these companies are stronger than ever. I'm not talking about the usual suspects like Apple, Starbucks, Google, or Southwest Airlines. I'm talking about small to midsize organizations like yours and mine, organizations that have managed to do more than just keep their heads above water during stormy times. They've sailed right through.

It's hard to believe this sort of growth is possible, given the bleak economic landscape. But I know it is happening, because I've spent the entire recession watching it with my own eyes. My team and I have spent the last eleven years guiding more than 400 businesses toward improving their performance in difficult times. These businesses are fortunate to have leaders who decided, as one CEO put it, that they simply were not going to participate in the recession. No matter what else was happening outside the gates, inside their offices, stores, and plants, these leaders decided to take ownership and to eliminate excuses by doing everything in their power to stay strong.

We've all seen, in recent years, executives who used the economy as an excuse for their own poor management, weak leadership, and bad decisions. Given the fact that the government has, in many ways, created and worsened this mess, it's an easy sell. The next step for these executives is to explain that they're waiting on the government to get us out. I, for one, don't buy it, and I've been lucky to work with leaders who decided they didn't want to wait

1   Carl Bialik, "Sizing Up the Small-business Jobs Machine," *Wall Street Journal*, 15 Oct. 2011, accessed 11 Jan. 2012, http://online.wsj.com/article/SB10001424052 970203914304576630973840478808.html.

2   Scott Shane, "Small Business Job Creation Is Stronger Than We Think," *Bloomberg Business Week*, 26 Apr. 2012, accessed 11 Jan. 2012, http://www.businessweek. com/articles/2012-04-26/small-business-job-creation-is-stronger-than-we-think.

for a government fix, either. I also put little stock in whether one party or another is running the White House. As we all know, and as has become painfully obvious in the last few years, the far reaches of government have hurt our economy in ways that go well beyond the Oval Office. From weak regulatory agencies to the self-interest of Congress, I believe those who pin their hopes on the presidential election are bound to be disappointed no matter who the winner is. I stand with those who say, "No excuses, no matter what." And I'm here to tell you there is a better exit strategy from the recession than remaining in a hiring freeze, cutting benefits, and slashing R&D spending, especially when—thanks to the efforts of small to midsize businesses around the country—conditions are warming up for a brighter business outlook.

The Steps That Will Make it Happen

As a voracious reader, I estimate that I've read somewhere in the neighborhood of 400 books on business, management, sales, and consulting. Many of them have shaped the philosophies and practices I apply in my own business. But with all due respect, something has been missing from all these books. I've been waiting for someone to give me a how-to guide for growing a small to midsize business in difficult economic times, a hands-on manual with a sensible philosophy and real-world examples to which I could relate. Nobody has delivered the goods. So I decided to write the business book that I would most like to read—and this is it.

To me, to Grow Regardless™ means to get in the arena and make it happen by joining the game. We have plenty of pundits and naysayers who would rather sit back and nitpick over the performance of those on the field, but often, that serves to destroy and tear down rather than to create and build up. Companies become mission-driven growth organizations by ignoring such distractions and focusing one hundred percent on the desired outcome and the journey it takes to get there. If there is one thing I learned growing up in the inner-city of Baltimore, it's that you can always find someone who's willing to drag you down, but if you seek a hand-up, you can always find people who are willing to do that, too. I wrote this book to help business leaders give themselves a hand up and then to turn around and extend that same boost to their employees, their customers, and their communities.

As CEO and co-founder of entreQuest (eQ), a Baltimore-based management consulting firm that helps increase revenue for small to midsize organizations, I have been helping companies grow since 2001. Over the years, the eQ team has developed and helped our client companies implement a simple growth methodology that works even during the worst of times. Our philosophy is backed by sensible processes and practical tactics that, when applied consistently, will bring about positive change and spur progress. Some of these concepts have been used by the "big guys" for years, but smaller enterprises can really rock by putting them into practice.

We call this method **The eQ Growth Methodology**. This is not a one-hit wonder. I didn't win the lottery and then decide to write a book about business growth. I didn't cash out with one big company or multiple companies because I am some crazy genius. I didn't get an MBA from an Ivy League school. At the age of twenty-three, I co-founded eQ, which grew to a multi-million-dollar practice just five years later. Today, companies pay us upward of $50,000-a-month to walk them through this process. We're going to spend the next several chapters exploring how you can apply this proven method to generate growth in your business.

Every year, thousands of books are published on sales, leadership, customer service, change management, and the like. They all say pretty much the same thing packaged in a different ways. A few things make *Grow Regardless* different. The first is its focus on mindset. Rather than just handing you a superficial to-do list, this book will teach you the mindset fundamentals necessary to grow your business and how to infuse that mentality throughout your organization. Getting your whole team to stand shoulder-to-shoulder on the same conceptual platform is critical to your success, and I'll show you exactly how to do that.

Another distinction of this book is the comprehensive way the information is presented. I've given each component of **The eQ Growth Methodology** its own chapter and explained it from the top-down using the Three Ps: ***philosophy*** for the thinkers and creative types among us, ***process*** for the managers and engineers, and ***practice*** for all the doers, practitioners, technicians, and front-line folks. The methodology will make sense to you—and actually work for you—because it's intuitive. Again, it all goes back to mindset. Full implementation cannot occur until everyone in your organization understands not only the *what* and the *how* of the method, but also the *why*. By understanding the Three Ps for each component, you'll be able to absorb them more quickly and communicate them to your team more effectively. I've even included practical exercises you can use to fully immerse yourself and your team in these concepts.

Grow Regardless references many of the best books and research ever done on change management and growth strategies, but I'm also going to tell you true stories of companies and people, including myself, that illustrate how these concepts are bearing real-world fruit for the leaders and organizations that adopt them. Those who know me know that it's not easy for me to write about myself, but I chose to share my stories to show that just as my experiences led to growth, yours have led you to a place of potential growth, too. When I thought about the purpose of this book—to help leaders of small to midsize businesses grow regardless—I realized my stories prove that if I can do this, anyone can.

In the chapters that follow, you'll also meet five outstanding leaders who have committed to do the work necessary to create mission-driven, growth organizations. Their stories shed light on practical approaches to leadership that can inspire all of us to make healthier, more reflective decisions:

- David Zdrojewski and John Walden have managed to grow their small manufacturing company, VibrAlign, through some of the most sluggish economic times in history using **The eQ Growth Methodology**. In fact, they just celebrated one of their best years ever after more than three decades in business. John and David are a testament to what it takes to make a true partnership work within a small company that is determined to do the right thing in a big way, despite the cards being stacked against them.
- Chris Krause is the founder and CEO of the National Collegiate Scouting Association (NCSA), a resource for student-athletes and their families in the college recruiting and scholarship process.

NCSA started with two employees and now has more than 300. That level of growth, which Krause and his team achieved rapidly, presented challenges in keeping the team connected and, most importantly, in tune with the company's culture. Today, NCSA is on track to become a $50 million company. Yet Krause has remained dedicated and consistent in maintaining and protecting the company's core values and culture throughout the organization.

- Oliver Carr is the CEO of Carr Workplaces, a Washington, DC-based company that provides serviced office space, virtual offices and meeting space to independent work groups and individuals. Oliver recognized early that the market was failing to serve the small business professionals who had a need for real estate space, and he helped to build the company on the premise of outstanding client service tailored to the unique requirements of this group. The company has flourished. Most strikingly, it has created a real sense of community among the individuals who work in its buildings.

- Doug Beigel is the award-winning CEO of COLA, a not-for-profit, physician-directed organization in Columbia, Maryland, that offers training, accreditation and consultation to medical labs to improve patient care. Being at the epicenter of the healthcare debate and fighting against the federal government for its very life, COLA had to find a way to continue its mission of increasing patient safety and enhancing the quality of healthcare in a time of diminished resources and industry volatility. Inspired by Doug's steady leadership, COLA's employees have learned to view themselves as the company's most important assets, and that has translated into growth.

Each of these leaders has mastered different components of **The eQ Growth Methodology** and put them into practice to make things better for themselves, their teams, and their customers. They each represent different sectors of the economy: nonprofit and privately-held small business. That's important, because it's going to take these segments along with publicly traded and privately owned, venture-backed organizations to work together to achieve true growth in this country. I also chose this diversity to demonstrate that you can grow no matter what type of company you have.

I decided to feature these individuals because they are passionate, high-integrity representatives of the small to midsize marketplace who have a story to tell. Their stories don't necessarily end with a $100-billion-revenue increase, but they are, without a doubt, stories of success in the journey toward becoming a mission-driven growth organization. John, David, Chris, Oliver, and Doug are more than just business leaders. They are growth personified. They are the embodiment of leadership through difficult times. They represent what twenty-first-century business in the United States is all about.

The eQ Growth Methodology starts with an initiative that helps companies take the first steps on the road to growth, and we call it "reset." It's the challenging—and powerful—process of undertaking an honest appraisal of yourself and your company and doing whatever it takes to set things right with your employees and your customers. Reset enables companies to learn from the past, accept it, and move on with a renewed (perhaps even a brand-new) commitment to doing what is best for your team, your company, your customers, and your community.

We follow this step by helping companies build—and, most importantly, sustain—the three pillars, which can make the difference between a business that thrives and a business that merely limps along, eventually falling to the next economic downturn or a shift in industry. First, companies must develop a compelling story that effectively conveys to clients and employees the authentic, values-driven reasons *why* they do what they do. Knowing the *what* and the *how* of your business is not enough; only by identifying your company's more pertinent reasons for being can you truly compel your team to achieve something greater than themselves.

The next step is to create an outstanding experience for your employees, because these are the people who can live out your story— or not—as they interact with your customers daily. Employees can be your best ambassadors or they can undermine leadership's efforts at every turn. In this economy, employers can no longer afford to ignore this key stakeholder in a company's success.

The third step is to create a remarkable experience for clients. This requires understanding that meeting or even exceeding expectations may no longer be enough. Give your clients a remarkable experience and you inspire a word-of-mouth sales force and long-term loyalty that complex growth strategies can't even touch.

So, build your story, hold yourself accountable to live out that promise every day, empower your employees to live out that promise, and commit to deliver that promise to your customers—it's a powerful combination that we have seen take companies to incredible heights. It sounds simple, and it is true that the principles that sustain **The eQ Growth Methodology** are not complex. But they do require a degree consistency and dedication to which some business leaders are unwilling to commit. Is the payoff worth the investment of your and your team's time, energy, effort and focus? I can unequivocally answer yes, it is, because I've put these principles to work in my own company, and I've seen them succeed hundreds of times with our clients.

I wrote this book with a practical application in mind, so it walks readers through **The eQ Growth Methodology** step by step. We'll talk about how to use the "25 Reasons Why" exercise to build your company's story; the seven qualities you must create in your workplace to create a great employee experience and inspire the level of performance that growth requires; straightforward steps you can take today to give your clients a remarkable experience; and, finally, the three components every entrepreneur can use to grow regardless.

I know it's scary out there. Plenty of small business owners and entrepreneurs have been living a horror story, with villains on every page. But here's the thing: There's a hero in this story, too. And that hero is you.

> You have the power to grow regardless of your company's size. You have the ability to grow regardless of your company's industry.
>
> You have the potential to grow regardless of the economy—and despite the stranglehold placed upon it by government.
>
> And you don't have to sell your soul to do it.

You have the capacity to influence others and start a movement that makes life better for everyone in America. It's time to sidestep our governmental gridlock, link arms, get completely honest with ourselves and each other, and do the right thing, which is to make meaningful promises to ourselves, our employees, our clients, our neighbors, and our families—and then to keep our word, no matter what. The time has come to find our voice as a group. Leaders of small to midsize businesses have the potential to drive this country's economy, and it's high time we started acting like it. It's going to take our combined heart, hustle, and humility to break through to the other side, but we can do it. Not only will we come out of the process better people than we were going in, but we'll also bootstrap our nation's recovery.

I believe the firsthand stories and simple strategies contained within these pages will move us closer to that worthy goal. These principles have the power to transform ordinary businesses into mission-driven growth organizations, and that has the power to change communities.

This is our movement: Helping companies *Grow Regardless*.

Study this book. Apply its principles. Pass it on. Grow Regardless.

Part One:

CLEARING THE WAY FOR GROWTH REGARDLESS

Chapter 1

THE METHOD
AND ME—
HUMBLE ORIGINS

The majority of men are bundles of beginnings.
—Ralph Waldo Emerson

I t was the summer of 1990 and I was thirteen years old, pounding the Baltimore pavement in search of a job. I was desperate for money. I had just had a big blowout with my mother and moved in with my dad.

My parents married young because I was on the way, and they were long divorced by this time. Dad, the hardest working man I have ever known, worked in a warehouse as a forklift driver. Mom was an aspiring actress who, as bright and lovely as she was, found it impossible to keep a conventional day job. Mom spent much of her time auditioning for television commercials and movie extra roles—for which she was rarely chosen. Consequently, she and I bounced around from place to place, house to house, and sofa to sofa for more than a decade, never actually homeless and starving but never stable, either. I attended five different schools in as many years, and I became a pro at recycling the few outfits we bought at Goodwill so I never had to wear the same combination of pants and shirt two days in a row. By the time I was a teenager, I was sick and tired of being broke and fed up with having no control over my life. Like most teenagers, I didn't want to rely on my dad or my mom anymore. I wanted to be independent and self-sufficient.

So that summer, while other kids my age were hanging out at the community swimming pool and playing ball in the sandlot, I was tramping up and down Eastern Avenue, cold-calling every gas station, convenience store, market, shop, and warehouse begging for work. It was hard for me to walk up to total strangers and ask for a job. I was painfully shy, and so much was riding on their answer. I must have gone to twenty-five places and talked to dozens of people, and everyone said no—except for the manager of a bakery. When I asked if he had a job for me, he said with a snort, "You want a job? Come back tomorrow at 4:30 a.m. and I'll put you to work."

I was so excited I practically flew the two blocks to our house. My dad, ever the pragmatist, was skeptical. But because he always supported me, he got up with me the next morning, drove me to the bakery at 4:30 a.m., and waited in the car to make sure everything was legit. The place was all lit up and workers, including the manager from the day before, bustling inside. I tried the door, but it was locked. I tapped on the glass and the workers and the manager looked up. I smiled and waved. When the manager saw me, he smirked, said something to the other people, and turned his back to me. I knocked again, but they all ignored me.

That bakery manager saw me, a timid kid, standing there tapping at his door at 4:30 a.m., but he decided not to let me in. That incident started me thinking that when you're in business and you promise something to someone, you've got to keep your word, no matter what. Whether you keep your word tells the story of who you are and where you're going in business and in life. It turns out this was only the first of many times I watched a company make a promise and then break it.

That bakery, by the way, has since gone out of business. I like to think it was because karma kicked them to the curb, but who am I to say?

Not long afterward, my dad ran into the man he used to work for when he was a teenager. Dad asked his former boss if he knew anyone who might give me a job. The man replied, "If your son is half the worker you are, I'll hire him myself."

So it was, that I went to work for Leo's Seafood, a Baltimore institution since the 1950s. Leo's had everything: seafood and grocery markets, a restaurant, a liquor store, and poker machines in the back—a true one-stop shop for the people of our blue-collar neighborhood. Working at Leo's was a big adjustment. I was a city boy who had never even touched a fish, let alone cleaned one. Suddenly, I had to clean them for paying customers. I was also extremely shy, and at Leo's I had to wait on customers face-to-face. There was no official hierarchy among the workers, but we all knew who our leader was: an elderly gentleman named Robert Butler. Robert was a quiet, unassuming man from the Deep South. He mumbled when he talked and shuffled when he walked. He moved as slow as molasses, but I'll be damned if every single customer who came to the seafood counter wanted Robert— and only Robert—to wait on them.

Even though I'm shy, I've always been fairly competitive, and I wanted more customers to choose me. I started watching the way Robert interacted with people, and what I saw was contrary to everything I thought I knew about customer service. I thought people would want to be waited on quickly, but I learned that what people really wanted was to be waited on *right*. Robert took the time to pick out the fattest, freshest crabs, and he'd throw in a couple of extra ones for his best customers. He'd fill a bag with ice to keep the seafood chilled all the way home, and he'd personally walk his customers to the checkout line, asking how they were and inquiring about their children or a sick mother. Meanwhile, people lined up ten deep at the seafood counter, and none of them wanted anything to do with me. They preferred to wait for Robert, who was moseying along with his current customer, rehashing last night's Orioles game.

People came to Leo's for a *product*, and they left with that product, but they also left with something extra: Robert's unconditional guarantee that if something wasn't right, he would fix it. They knew he would be there for them no matter what—he would keep his word.

Eventually, after watching and learning from Robert, I started to earn a few loyal customers of my own. I worked my way into their hearts by imitating the little things Robert did to exceed their expectations. Once I had learned how to communicate that same sense of caring and accountability to our customers, more of them started to choose me.

I worked at the seafood market for seven years, every weekend of my teens. I learned about hard work and being part of a team. But more important, I learned about the client experience. This is where I started to understand that by giving everything and more to your customers, you get really good things in return . . . such as referrals and repeat business. You get growth.

Unfortunately, this story doesn't have a great ending for Leo's. As the economy soured, the company hit hard times and began grasping at straws to survive. The store tried to diversify too much too quickly. We started catering big jobs and parties, which diverted our focus from the neighborhood folks who were our bread and butter. Leo's eventually closed after more than fifty years in business. Those of us who worked there learned the hard lesson that nothing is permanent. You have to take care of your customers if you want to last.

 You have to take care of your customers if you want to last.

Because I wanted to make more money than I was earning at Leo's, I once took a second job at a gourmet grocery store famous for its outstanding customer service. It was true that the market was an amazing place to shop. But it was a terrible place to work. If you were a few seconds late returning from your break, or you didn't tie your tie correctly, or you didn't greet every customer with the same canned line, the manager nailed you to the wall. The workers had no authenticity or passion. They were well-programmed robots with a check-the-box mentality. I quit after three weeks, but it was one of the most valuable jobs I have ever had, because I learned that it wasn't enough to provide a remarkable customer experience. You have to provide a quality *employee* experience, too. If that market had treated its employees as well as it did its customers, it would have been exponentially more successful.

I attended Baltimore's Patterson High School, which was a pretty dismal place. More than 900 kids were in my freshman class, but only 235 of us graduated. Because I was a decent football player, I was recruited by Johns Hopkins University. Going from one of the worst high schools in the state to one of the best colleges in the world was a culture shock. I floundered a bit, changing my major from engineering to pre-med and back to engineering, finally settling on economics because I could talk my way through that. Somehow I did okay.

At the beginning of my sophomore year, I received a flyer in the mail that read: *Do you want to run your own business?* Check. *Do you want to earn college credit?* Check. *Do you want to make $10,000 this summer?* That was five times more than I had earned the previous summer, so . . . check!

The flyer came from a company that recruited college kids and taught them how to run their own painting franchises. Once trained, it was up to you to staff your team and find your own jobs. I signed on and went through the training. My first year was tough, like the first year of any new business. I hired a bunch of friends and then had to fire some of them because they rarely listened to anything I said. But because of what I'd learned by watching Robert at the seafood market all those years, we gave great customer service. And just like at the seafood market, I saw that the better the customer service, the more money we made.

By my second summer running the business, I had read Michael E. Gerber's *The E Myth*, which explored the importance of making a promise to your customers and telling them a compelling story about yourself. So instead of just saying that we had a painting business, we told people we were working for our college tuition—we wanted to work hard and earn a fair wage by providing a service people needed. All of a sudden, our sales more than doubled. I went from having half a dozen employees to more than fifty, all by changing the way I positioned our story and by doubling down on client service. My teams showed up clean and on time. On the first day of a new job, we brought coffee and donuts for the client. If we didn't finish on time, we refunded some of the money. When there was a problem, we fixed it. We cleaned up the job site when we left each day. We weren't the best painters by a long stretch, but because we were sincere and we tried so hard, people were nice to us and told their friends about us.

By the third year, I had more than a hundred people working for me. I made more money that summer than many people make today in a year. But there were problems at the corporate level that I wasn't aware of, and one day the company was unable to meet its obligations. I had a group of guys painting at a mansion near the Johns Hopkins campus, and when they found out what was happening with the company, they decided to get back at corporate. They trashed the mansion. They broke windows and threw black oil-based paint all over the place. The owner, Stan Burns, was understandably upset. He tried to get company officials to fix the damage, but just got the runaround. I went to see Stan and reassured him that I would send a new crew over to make repairs the following week, and I'd pay them out of my own pocket. He refused.

"No, I want *you* to fix it," Stan said. "You, personally."

Me? Personally? Was this guy crazy? I was only running this business; I didn't know how to paint! I told Stan that, and I also told him I was scheduled to fly out of Baltimore in a few days to start a new job at one of the top consulting firms in the nation. Stan was unmoved. He insisted I take personal responsibility for righting the mess my crew had made.

Well, what else could I do? I had to keep my word.

So I showed up at Stan's house bright and early the next morning and went to work. My progress was so slow, and I had to postpone the start of my new job. I had labored several hours each day for a couple of weeks when one afternoon around lunchtime, Stan popped into the room where I was working and invited me to go out for a sandwich. That was the first of many lunches we shared over the following months. Stan, who had recently retired as president of Chase Bank of Maryland, had been an incredibly successful businessman. He was a popular consultant who wrote books and articles for business journals. He had even thrown out the first pitch at Major League baseball games. He was a rock star in the business world.

In short, Stan was quite a guy, and for some reason he liked me. He took me under his wing and shared his philosophies on life and business. We talked about how to be a good man, a good husband, and a good father. From Stan, I learned that to be successful, you have to follow what you're passionate about.

> You've got to love who you work with and love who you do the work for. That's the kind of passion that breeds success.
> —Stan Burns

Stan helped me to see that my passion did not lie in working for the prestigious consulting firm that had made me a generous offer at the end of college. With my blue-collar background, I probably wouldn't have been happy there. I didn't come with the kind of pedigree so prevalent in a company like that. I don't button my sleeves or tuck in my shirt. I would have been a square peg trying to fit into a round hole.

Instead, I wanted to serve as a teacher and a leader for small and midsize companies, companies whose values and histories closely aligned with my own, companies that were mission-driven and growth-oriented. Stan opened my eyes to that. In granting me permission to break the rules and adjust my aspirations, he gave me an incredible gift.

About six months later, I met the partner with whom I started entreQuest, and the rest, as they say, is history.

Stan was a generous person whose wisdom and encouragement changed the trajectory of my life forever. He had perfected the use of story in business—in fact, he had written a book titled *Exceeding Expectations: The Enterprise Rent-A-Car Story*—and he passed that concept on to me. Since then, I have implemented that concept to help build what would become my own multi-million-dollar company. Stan's legacy lives on in my company and in all the entrepreneurs entreQuest has helped over the years, including the five incredible leaders you're going to meet in later chapters.

Chapter 2

UNDERSTANDING OUR NEW-NEW REALITY

A pessimist sees the difficulty in every opportunity;
an optimist sees the opportunity in every difficulty.
—Winston Churchill

To say we have a challenging economy is an understatement. If you listen to the experts, you'll believe that what we're experiencing is nothing more than a replay of tough times past. The 2008–2009 recession, they say, wasn't another Great Depression in the making, but it was part of the natural economic cycle. All the same, our situation differs dramatically from any other downturn to date.

Our society is more complex than ever before. Technology has revolutionized virtually everything about the way we do business and the way we interact. We ourselves have changed, both individually and collectively. We have new skill sets, shifting demographics, and evolving values.

In this environment, the challenge before us is that for every new strength we have gained, there is an equal and opposite weakness. Take the

Internet, for example—undeniable, the online universe delivers a powerful capacity to expand our business models and our reaches. On the other hand, this same technology can disconnect us from our customers and distract us in our pursuits. The financial underpinnings of our economy are similarly dualistic. Our nation's appetite for credit has enabled growth and acquisition, but careless debt, as we have seen, has burdened us with an economy built dangerously on sand.

The successful business leader recognizes these dynamics and the need for balance. It is important to understand where we are today as a result of debt, disconnection, and distraction, so we can then learn how to harness the positive potential on the other side of the coin.

Bear in mind, too, that after the Great Depression, there was one big thing our country had going for it that it doesn't have now. Back then, when the time came to put people to work, there were plenty of industrial jobs to step into. That's not the case anymore.

To grow regardless, we must accept these realities and draw upon that understanding to develop a fresh mindset. We can then harness the power of **The eQ Growth Methodology** and use these new realities to our advantage going forward.

Debt

Remember *Good to Great: Why Some Companies Make the Leap . . . and Others Don't*, Jim Collins' blockbuster book from 2001? Collins researched American corporations, identified eleven whose stock significantly outperformed the market and examined why they did so much better than their competitors. These eleven companies were supposed to be the best of the best. Among those Collins held up as superior models of corporate greatness were Fannie Mae and Circuit City. In case you missed the headlines, Fannie Mae was put into a government conservatorship in 2008 as a result of its starring role in the massive home mortgage scandal, and Circuit City went bankrupt.

So what's an author to do when he calls it wrong? Write another book, of course! Collins answered *Good to Great* with *How the Mighty Fall*, in which he examines the five stages of corporate decline. Collins names "hubris born of success" as the first stage, citing a lack of caution and awareness as a key reason for failure. I agree wholeheartedly. Later we'll take a close look at awareness; because for a leader, a team, or a company to succeed, there must be a profound awareness of self and surroundings and an ongoing, candid assessment of both. For now, suffice it to say that in recent years, America has dropped the ball on both caution and awareness. We have been blinded by our success and feel entitled to have more. Our "too big to fail" mentality, if left unchecked, threatens to hobble us going forward.

This lack of discipline shows up in the fact that our assets are leveraged to the maximum. Seeking to acquire even more, we've leveraged practically everything in our lives—our relationships, time, homes, and technology— to bump up our return and turn something small into something big. Our mantra has become: "Buy now, pay tomorrow." Yet instead of creating more options with our newfound success, we often end up with more headaches. Meanwhile, other countries are using technology to surpass us in education and other areas of achievement.

According to the Federal Reserve, Americans owed a staggering $2.57 trillion in consumer credit in the second quarter of 2012. Consumer credit increased at an annual rate of 5 percent in the same quarter.[3] Apparently, the lessons of the economic downturn have gone largely unheeded.

It's time to start de-leveraging and investing heavily in our current assets. This will be a slow and painful process. It could take a decade to get back to a healthy, pre-recession leverage intensity. It's going to mean less output and potentially less spending for a while, which will certainly impact our recovery. But we have little choice, because our former path is unsustainable. This doesn't mean we can't grow; it just means we may grow less than we hoped when we first launched into unfettered leveraging. As I see it, using our assets more wisely may simply mean that we grow *differently*.

If we expect to grow regardless, we must give ourselves more options. How? Become more aware, and learn to do more with less. Or, as my mentor Steve Lishansky, founder and president of Optimize International, says, "It's

---

3   Federal Reserve, Consumer Credit-G.19, 7 Aug. 2012, accessed 30 Aug. 2012, http://www.federalreserve.gov/Releases/g19/Current/.

not doing more with less, but the less that matters more." These are not just clichés, but new laws. Eating what you kill is the new reality. Eating what you kill is about personal accountability and a "no handouts" mentality: *If I'm not willing to kill it, I shouldn't expect to eat it.* Because as much as we are all in this together, we're all in this alone, too. Once we accept that, we will have the sense of urgency it will take to win consistently.

 As my mentor Steve Lishansky says, "It's not doing more with less, but the less that matters more."

Everyone has a bad day now and then. But to survive in this economy, you have to create and maintain a sense of urgency for yourself and your team. As Americans, we tend to fall back on one of two mindsets: *I will beat everyone* or *I can pull through in the end.* What we fall back on less readily is the mindset of working hard, expecting no frills, and watching good things happen as a result.

That's what folks did during the Great Depression. Those who made money were those who outworked everybody else. So here's another cliché with which to get reacquainted: the early bird catches the worm. Your competitors are hustling more than ever to grab their fair share, and there will be less to go around. If people are spending less, how can you grow regardless? Economics 101 says that when supply goes down, demand goes up. If demand goes up, pricing and competition intensify, creating more value in every interaction and every transaction. That doesn't mean you can't grow. It just means that growth may demand that your team build new skills. Only those who are the best at what they do and offer the most value to the marketplace will succeed.

Underlying these factors is another wrinkle in our societal cloth, and it's a biggie: our economy has shifted into an entirely different realm. Whereas we once relied on agriculture (farmers), manufacturing (factory workers), and information (knowledge workers) to drive our economy, we are now entering the Age of the Creator. In his excellent book, *A Whole New Mind: Why Right-Brainers Will Rule the Future*, Daniel H. Pink observes that for the last decade or so, the people who have led the way in business have been *creators*, not creators in the typical sense of manufacturing, although that's still important. I'm talking about the creation of things you can't touch, like Facebook and Google. Today's creators provide us solutions to problems we don't even know we had. In a sense, they are artists. Put bluntly, the people who carried us to this point in history couldn't get us out of this mess if we wanted them to. It's now up to the creative class. If we're to prevail, we need to take our cue from them, working harder and, more importantly, thinking differently than ever before.

Innovators today can create information, a pathway to success, and a new approach to old things. They can create an entirely new way to book a flight, serve clients, or stay connected with relatives across the country. New approaches are less about coming up with *the* way to do something and more about devising all the many ways you *can* do something. It's a stunningly different mentality. The good news is that creativity is based more on life experience, learning, and a novel approach than on IQ, which means that anyone has the capacity for it. And the one thing that drives creation more than anything else is something for which we can all be grateful: the Internet.

Distracted

The Internet is the single biggest innovation of all time, period. We are unbelievably lucky to be witnessing the expansion of this new technological frontier. If you were to look back on our history during the advent of the automobile or the First Transcontinental Railroad, you might wonder why our ancestors didn't see the full potential of what was happening right under their noses. I predict that one day the same will be said of us.

Our co-existence with the Internet reminds me of the old story of the boiling frog. If you toss a frog into a pot of boiling water, it'll jump right out. But if you put a frog into cool water and gently turn up the heat, the frog will sit there until it cooks. The heat increase is so gradual that the frog feels no urgency to jump out of the pot. We aren't so different. An entire generation was thrown into the Internet pot, and we barely notice its massive impact on every aspect of our lives.

Like any tool, the Internet can become a detriment if used unwisely. On a personal level, many of us can relate to the phenomenon that while the Internet is our biggest ally in productivity, it is also our biggest time-waster. As a commercial tool, we can leverage the Internet to open new markets, engage with customers to an unprecedented degree, improve service, and generally raise the bar. If we aren't careful, though, the Internet becomes a distraction and a disconnection. We may rely too heavily on the Internet to handle customers, forgetting that there are actual human beings on the other end of the transaction. If staff is not proactively trained otherwise, the loss of face-to-face interaction can have a dampening effect on the way we treat customers, vendors, and even colleagues.

Another challenge is that we have become so accustomed to the power of the Internet to expand our capabilities and improve our lives that many of us don't actively explore how the Internet can help us professionally. Among other factors, we've never had this many choices from a goods and services perspective. Twenty years ago, my options for buying a new jacket were the four clothing stores within driving distance of my house. Now I have access to countless stores online—and so do your customers. The ball is in the consumers' court. Remember earlier in this chapter when we talked about how pricing and competition intensify when people are making and spending less? That puts the ball even *more* firmly in the buyers' court because when they have less to spend, their eye for quality goes up, their expectations rise considerably, and they are more attentive to value. That means providers must fight even harder to keep their business.

The Internet has the potential to level the playing field for every consumer, and it can do the same for you. The Internet cannot only provide information and intelligence about your market and your consumer, it can help you reach them for free. In the late 1990s, you might have had to spend $200,000 to do half of what Facebook does today for free. Skype is free. LinkedIn is free. YouTube is free. You can't even take an extra bag on an airplane for free. It's mind-blowing when you stop and think about it.

Only those business leaders with the knowledge and skill to use the Internet to its fullest potential—without allowing it to introduce negative outcomes—will be able to grow regardless; everyone else will be left behind, eating dust. It's just that simple.

Disconnected

A key part of delighting your customers and inspiring your employees is being able to understand what motivates them. This isn't as straightforward as you might think, as shown in a 2005 study by economists at the Massachusetts Institute of Technology, Carnegie-Mellon and the University of Chicago.[4] Researchers gave students a set of tasks to complete—shooting a basketball through a hoop, memorizing a string of numbers, and solving word puzzles—and offered three levels of monetary rewards. If participants did the task sort of well, they got a little money. If they performed somewhat better, they got more money; and if they were among the best at a task, they got even more money. This is the way things usually work in our companies, right? We pay the top performers more and we disregard the bottom tier.

But check this out. The researchers found that as the tasks required more thought and creativity, and offered the promise of a bigger reward, *the poorer the performance*. What motivates people to be more creative (and remember, creativity is what's going to drive our economy and help us grow regardless) is to pay them enough that they can focus on their work without having to worry about their finances. Pink suggests that employers who want to motivate creativity should not only pay people a fair wage and appropriate bonuses, but also help them fulfill three desires: for autonomy, mastery, and a higher purpose. Autonomy is the need to be self-directed in controlling our time. Mastery is the innate desire to perform at a progressively higher level. Purpose is the hope of contributing something to the greater good.

Psychologist and author Daniel Goleman says that while IQ is a great predictor of how high a position one can attain in a career, it may not be the best predictor of *leadership success*. A person's emotional intelligence

---

4   Dan Ariely et al., "Large Stakes and Big Mistakes," Working Papers, Federal Reserve Bank of Boston, 23 July 2005, accessed 29 Nov. 2011, http://www.bos.frb.org/economic/wp/wp2005/wp0511.pdf.

(commonly called EQ, for emotional quotient) also plays an important role.[5] EQ is the ability to recognize, gauge, and control your emotions and to recognize and respond to those of other people. According to Goleman's research, EQ has four dimensions: self-awareness, social awareness, emotional management, and relationship management.

Goleman's conclusions play out in the workplace every day, as demonstrated in a 2011 CareerBuilder poll of 2,662 US hiring managers[6]:

- An overwhelming 71 percent value EQ in an employee more than IQ.
- Almost 60 percent of employers would not hire someone with a high IQ but low EQ.
- Among workers being considered for promotion, the candidate with high EQ will beat out the high IQ candidate 75 percent of the time.

Without a doubt, research supports the notion that EQ is an important ingredient for success. How do you know if you have a high EQ? You spend a lot of time asking yourself questions like *What can I learn from this? What is going to be great about today? What will help me have a positive impact on people?* You allow yourself to have those creative thoughts. You respond, instead of reacting. When you have a high EQ, you take personal responsibility. You ask yourself how *you* can improve a situation. You conduct an honest self-appraisal of your role in contributing to challenges around you. You recognize that you can't always control an event, but you can control your response. Others come to you for advice because they're confident you are willing and able to offer value. If you don't get too many of those kinds of phone calls, you need to think about beefing up your EQ, because you've created an energy around you that is not conducive to growth.

---

5   Daniel Goleman, *Emotional Intelligence: Why It Can Matter More Than IQ*, 10th Anniv. Ed., New York: Bantam, 2006, xiii-xiv.

6   CareerBuilder, Press Release, 18 Aug. 2011, accessed 28 Nov. 2011, http://www. careerbuilder.com/share/aboutus/pressreleasesdetail.aspx?id=pr652&sd=8/18/201 1&ed=08/18/2011,

The ability to genuinely connect with others—your customers and your teammates—will set you apart from the competition. Relationships matter. Anyone who tells you, "It's not personal, it's only business," is deluded. Just as all politics are local, all business is personal nowadays.

I emphasize that this applies equally to employees and customers. The common consensus has always been that clients come first and employees bring up the rear. I believe this is a lingering remnant of the second-class treatment of factory workers during the Industrial Age. Although things have improved markedly, it wasn't until the 1990s that employers had a real wake-up call. The economy exploded and the unemployment rate dropped as low as 2 or 3 percent. Suddenly, employees had as many options as consumers. Alert employers made adjustments that helped them attract and retain the best employees, such as better pay and benefits, profit sharing, onsite daycare, tuition assistance, and other perks. Not only did these companies receive positive PR for the way they treated their people, they also experienced greater productivity and profits.

The same cautions that apply to the Internet apply here to the interpersonal dynamics in organizations. As business leaders achieve the growth for which they have worked so hard, many of them are struggling to maintain the connection with employees that drove that growth in the first place. Recognizing the importance of this connection and striving to sustain it no matter how large a company becomes is critical.

Although you should be providing a remarkable experience for your people, keep in mind that it's all relative. A remarkable experience on an airline and a remarkable experience at Disney World are in two different categories. For customers, a remarkable experience on an airline would be: "They got me there on time; the workers were pleasant; I got complimentary champagne; the plane wasn't overbooked; and they didn't make me check my luggage." A remarkable experience at Disney World would be: "I've been there three times and they treated me like royalty every time; and I want it to be unbelievable yet again."

I look at employee experience the same way. Obviously, the bar is naturally lower for your employees than for your customers, but still, you should strive to treat your employees like your clients and your clients like your employees as much as you can. No one's going to argue that clients need a great experience, but many people might argue that in today's economy, we can afford to revert to the employer-employee dynamic of yesteryear because our people have fewer choices. I'm here to tell you that employable people have just as many choices as ever. It's the unemployable people who are going to have problems. Happy employees translate into happy customers, as you'll see later on when we meet an extraordinary CEO named Chris Krause.

In summary, here are our cold, hard new-new realities: We're an over-leveraged, overconfident society evolving to a creation-driven economy, supported and advised by people we don't understand and who don't always understand us, and supported by technology that we have yet to master. Read on for a proven growth method that addresses all of this.

Chapter 3

THE eQ
GROWTH
METHODOLOGY

*The seed must **grow, regardless***
Of the fact that it's planted in stone . . .
The flower blooms, with brilliance
And outshines the rays of the sun.
— **Tupac Shakur**

So, how can you grow regardless of your industry, your size, and the economy, and despite the government? It comes down to a few simple steps that any organization can take whether that organization is a small business, a nonprofit, or a publicly-traded company. I do mean simple. The method that we have helped hundreds of companies implement to successfully achieve growth consists of only four steps:

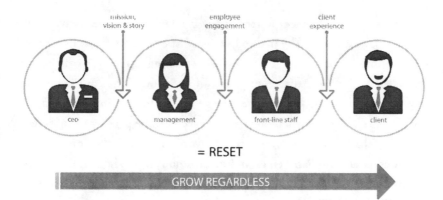

1. Hit the "reset" button, acknowledging the past and making reparations to move your company forward with a renewed commitment to your team, your customers, and your community.
2. Develop your company's story, which tells clients and employees alike not only *what* you do, but *why* you do it.
3. Do everything you can to make your employees feel like valued members of your team.
4. Create a remarkable experience for your clients—at every turn.

It's important to note that **The eQ Growth Methodology** isn't only for CEOs and other executives. It is applicable to anyone in the organization. Even a mid-level manager or frontline worker can employ this method to create meaningful change and spur growth wherever they are. In fact, my clients have heard me say over and over that this growth plan, like any business strategy, will succeed only to the degree that top leaders are effective in pushing the message throughout the entire organization. While the CEO may chart the course, he or she needs the entire crew to row in unison to reach the destination smoothly and efficiently.

Here's one more piece of good news: It doesn't matter if you didn't start your business this way. You can start to incorporate these principles at any point in your company's timeline.

The eQ Growth Methodology emphasizes process, practice, and execution. This stuff works. I've seen it work not only in my own little world but also in the diverse organizations we have worked with for eleven years.

In fact, one of our clients experienced 367 percent growth after only ninety days of focused effort. The method we prescribe is not a fancy marketing tactic, a trendy social media strategy, or a training course for your team; this is about transformation—of your culture, your relationships, and the way you do business. Because we believe in continuous improvement in response to change, our method takes into account the paradigms we talked about in Chapter 2: the current economy, the Internet, the complexities of contemporary human beings and our relationships. The cornerstone of our process is doing the right thing for your people, your company, and your **COMMUNITY**. Notice how I put the word "community" in caps, underlined, and in bold print. That's how important community is to your overall success in becoming a mission-driven organization.

So without further ado, meet your new growth methodology.

Growth Begins With Relationships

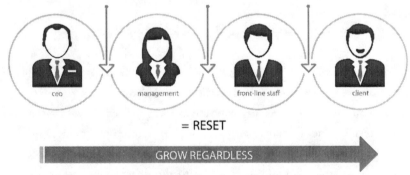

For all organizations of all sizes in all industries, growth is a function of the intersections between relationships.

Under the new-new reality, the way we interact with one another has changed. Between baby boomers and the millennial generation there is a vast landscape of new values, complex technology, and an increasingly tumultuous global economy. To grapple with these challenges, business people typically focus on improving processes, whether it's through a Six Sigma program, a better "go to market" strategy, or a new branding campaign. All of those can certainly be part of the solution, but one thing that is not talked about nearly enough is the importance of improving the connections between leadership, employees, and clients. I believe that establishing and maintaining healthy relationships is the missing link when it comes to spurring business growth.

In his bestselling book, *Competitive Advantage: Creating and Sustaining Superior Performance*, Michael Porter coined the term "value chain" to describe the sequence of activities that occur as an organization carries out its business. The focus is on what happens to the product as it travels the length of the chain from procurement to manufacture to sales to distribution. But what Porter's model misses is the fact that all along that value chain are *people*—people who relate to and interact with one another. It really is all about relationships. The dynamic between the CEO and the management team influences frontline staff, which ultimately impacts the client. Depending on the quality of these relationships, this impact can be either positive or negative, resulting in either growth or downsizing in the areas of revenue, profit, employees, client numbers, and client retention.

Today, you must consider everyone in the value chain as equals. Why limit yourself to having only your sales team do sales? **The eQ Growth Methodology** entails mobilizing everyone from your CEO, to the management team, to the front line, and to clients to become advocates for your organization. Anyone and everyone in and around your company can help it grow regardless, but first you have to understand how people think and feel. If everyone in and around your organization has a great experience, they're going to tell people. Remember, we buy today based on word-of-mouth in a way we never have before. There's less trust in the marketplace, less trust in the economy and less money to go around. So, while having a traditional sales team is great, imagine what might happen if you had a team of goodwill ambassadors for your company that extended all through that chain of relationships. You could exponentially increase the effort and get more referrals, more awareness, more brand recognition, and, ultimately, more growth.

The remaining chapters will show you exactly how to do that. For now, let's look at a brief overview of the components.

Today, you must consider everyone in the value chain as equals. Why limit yourself to only having your sales team do sales?

Hit the Reset Button

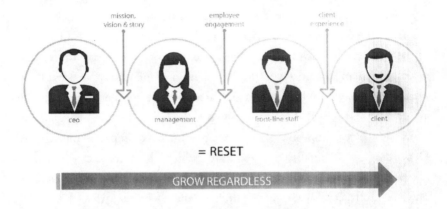

Transforming your company's story, your employees' and customers' experiences, and your culture starts by hitting reset. You start by acknowledging and accepting the past and your employees' and customers' points of view. In some cases, you may even find it necessary to apologize for the past. We don't say we're sorry often enough in business. A sincere apology can have a huge, positive impact on your entire organizational chain. Accept, acknowledge, and apologize—and then turn to face the sun. Leave yesterday behind and move on. I'll tell you how to do that effectively in Chapter Four.

Strengthened by Story

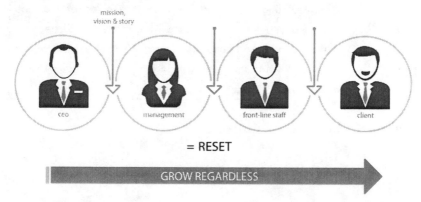

mission,
vision & story

ceo | management | front-line staff | client

= RESET

GROW REGARDLESS

A good company story is more than a few paragraphs outlining a mission statement. It speaks to history and values, what the company stands for, how it competes, and what it wants to be to its people and its clients. It communicates all of that in a unique, compelling manner that inspires employees, prospects, clients, and community. Remember Apple's "Think Different" commercial from the late 1990s in which actor Richard Dreyfus recited the poem "Here's to the Crazy Ones" while images of Albert Einstein, John Lennon, Dr. Martin Luther King, Jr., and other notable change-makers flashed across the screen? Apple's use of story in that ad captured the world's attention—and its technology dollars—in an extraordinary, enduring way. Not a single Apple product appeared in the ad, yet its debut marked a watershed moment in the company's history. Apple hasn't looked back since.

Your story defines your company's promise to the world and gets everyone on your team working together to live it out. In many ways, the story is a deeply-rooted belief, a psychological state that holds a proposition or premise to be true. People act based upon these kinds of deeply-rooted beliefs, and over time those individual acts add up to growth.

Creating such a story seems simple, but it takes time and effort to get it right. It also requires abandoning the previous stories or sagas that may have worked in past economic climates. We'll cover story in depth in Chapter 5.

According to a 52-week study of consumer loyalty in 2010–2011, Catalina Marketing reported that sales of the one hundred packaged-goods brands it tracked grew 2.2 percent. But if the brands had been able to maintain sales to customers who were loyal to their products in the past, their sales would have grown 8.5 percent, on average.[7]

Reinforced by Valued Employees

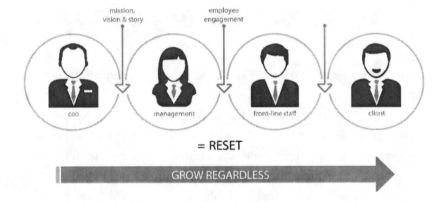

It's interesting that so many television shows recently have depicted an office environment in which the leader is arguably incompetent, but stays in charge by virtue of rank and title. Take one of my favorite shows, *The Office*. Jim, Pam, Dwight, Oscar, Phyllis, Angela, Kevin, and Stanley knew that it wasn't only Michael Scott's responsibility to make Dunder Mifflin's Scranton branch profitable. It was up to every one of them. As incompetent as Michael Scott was, he was great at getting buy-in from his people. The Scranton branch was successful because all the employees owned it.

That's the reason for this segment of **The eQ Growth Methodology**. Your employees are the ones who will be living out your story for your clients . . . or not. They are the ones who will keep your company's promises . . . or

---

7   Jack Neff, "Catalina: Major Packaged-Goods Brands Lost 46% of Loyalists," *Advertising Age*, 7 Sept. 2011, accessed 11 Jan. 2012, http://adage.com/article/news/catalina-major-packaged-goods-brands-lost-46-loyalists/229640/.

not. It's well established that satisfied employees equal growth. When you create an environment that enables and inspires employees to be personally invested in the health and well-being of the company, they will naturally support it. The opposite also is true. Employees who feel disenfranchised or disconnected are likely to give minimum effort, and no more. Chapter 6 is filled with practical tips and techniques for providing a great employee experience in a way that stimulates growth.

"[O]rganization culture is not a soft concept. Its impact on profit can be measured and quantified. And in organizations with large numbers of customer-facing employees, the sum of the effects of employee turnover, referrals of potential employees by existing ones, productivity, customer loyalty, and referrals of new customers attributable to culture *can add up to half of the difference in operating income between organizations in the same business.*"
—Harvard Business School Professor Emeritus **James Heskett**

And Sustained by Remarkable Client Experiences

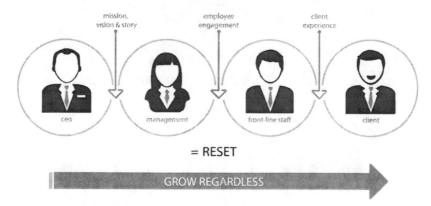

What I have to say about the client experience may not sound much different from other customer service books, except for one major distinction: I believe the level of priority and the amount of passion and emphasis that must be put toward the customer experience must be, in a word, unreasonable. It must be excessive. It must go beyond the limits of common sense. It must be extreme, irrational and out of proportion with what your competitors are doing. It cannot be anything less than *remarkable*. The client experience begins as a philosophy and aligns all employees with the relentless pursuit of ensuring the client consistently experiences exactly what you promised. As a result, clients can—and do!—express precisely why they buy your product or service. You end up with not only a good client who is willing to buy more from you, but also a client who is willing to refer others, an enthusiastic ambassador who feels compelled to speak highly of you. That's what you're aiming for.

So, as it turns out, the early department store magnates were one hundred percent correct when they said, "The customer is always right." You can use that philosophy to your advantage as long as you keep your word. Chapter 7 will show you how.

Part Two:

Nurturing Growth
Regardless

Chapter 4

HIT THE
RESET BUTTON

Progress lies not in enhancing what is,
but in advancing toward what will be.
—Kahlil Gibran

I'm a little reluctant to share this story, because the last thing a company that helps businesses grow should probably talk about is how they screwed it up themselves. But I believe in self-disclosure as long as it's for the greater good, so I'm going to swallow my pride and tell it like it is. Here goes:

entreQuest is not a large consulting company. We're not Bain. We're not FTI. We're certainly not of the Big Four variety. But within our own little world, we've been able to help a lot of companies grow, and consequently, we grew, too. In our first six years, eQ had a nice growth rate from an organizational perspective, about 33 percent annually. That's pretty good for a service-based company. As we began to grow, we began to diversify our thinking about how we would expand the business even more. We acquired a recruiting company. We began chasing a multi-million-dollar contract with a large software company. We continued to build prominence in our mid-Atlantic marketplace. We had our eyes wide open, always scanning the horizon for more opportunities.

But what we totally missed were the first tell-tale signs of a marketplace headed for disaster. It was early 2008. We did business with several companies in the housing sector, and we saw them begin to shake and crumble. But instead of reading the signs, instead of listening and having good self-awareness and good social awareness, we just kept putting all our eggs in a few baskets—the big software company contract and our recruiting business. We were in La-La Land.

In the first six months of 2008, we watched our recruiting division go from a large part of our business to virtually nothing. And that big software company contract we'd been chasing, the one for which we had several verbal agreements, the one that would have helped us scale to 110 companies across the country? At the last second, they turned to us and said, "No. We're not going to fund you." We had 30 percent of our recurring clients go away almost overnight because they were smack dab in the middle of the housing crisis. And on top of all that, we watched one of our clients go out of business and with that, a good amount of uncollectible accounts receivable. All this was in the first six months of 2008.

You might think this would have been a great time for us to hit the reset button, but we didn't. For the next ninety days we were shaken to the core—a herd of deer in headlights. Our company was losing in excess of $50,000 a month. We were in danger of complete collapse. Out of a total lack of awareness of ourselves and the marketplace, we decided to make one last-ditch effort. We made one of the non-founding partners the CEO for ninety days . . . and we continued on with the same old strategy. The only smart thing we did was to put a line in the sand that said if we weren't able to hit certain outcomes over those ninety days, we would restructure the company.

And that's what we ended up doing. In October of 2008, we laid-off more than half of our staff and made big changes in leadership. I hit a major reset button. It was one of the hardest things I've ever done.

Reset is not supposed to be about dire straits. It's not supposed to be done because you don't have any other option. You should actually do reset when you're winning. In other words, reset shouldn't be seen as a company's emergency flotation device, but rather its launching point for better business. It's like the reaction some of us have when we hear that a friend is going to therapy. There's a stigma attached, a feeling there must be something wrong with the person. In reality, it could be that your friend is simply making an investment in who they are—an investment in becoming a better human being. Reset is the same way.

The reset eQ went through in 2008 was more like rehab. There's nothing wrong with rehab, but you usually go there only when you've hit rock bottom. We had hit rock bottom. We were on life support. The company that had touted its ability to help companies grow regardless suddenly found itself having to hunker down, lick its wounds, and answer some really tough questions about who we are, why we exist and where we wanted to go.

For years, I had operated under the belief that if the market loved what we did—it would want more of our services, regardless of the economy. If that were true, and knowing that management consulting has been around for a hundred years and isn't going anywhere, then the conclusion I came to was an odd one indeed, given who we were and the fact that we had a lot of experience in this field.

The conclusion I came to was this: We weren't very good at what we did.

If we were not as good as we thought we were, and we needed to raise our game, what would that look like?

To find out, the first thing we did was go to every single client we had left and ask them, "How can we serve you better? What's been going wrong from your perspective?" Our mission was to expose the elephants, even if it was painful. In many cases, our clients kicked back excellent feedback. We learned that much of what we thought was going so well truly wasn't.

The second thing I did was go to my employees and ask them how they thought we ought to move forward. I was determined to allow people to participate in decision-making whenever it made sense. Sometimes I held a vote, sometimes I sought consensus, and sometimes I made decisions on my own, but I tried to be thoughtful about involving the team.

I also came to realize that all this surveying and consensus-seeking and vote-taking was good, but more important, it was impressing on my team that we were going to have to hustle like never before if we were going to beat our competition. I decided that we would become the most trained team ever. So, since 2008, our team has gathered every single Friday afternoon for anywhere from one to four hours and conducted self-training. We've brought in people from the outside. We've trained each other. We've had group discussions. We've brainstormed. We've collaborated. We've gotten out and volunteered in the community. We've consumed a bunch of beer. We've had a lot of great times together.

While some companies do this once a year, once a quarter or once a month, we've kept the commitment to regrouping every single week. My vision was that if we did this for three years straight, we could one day be recognized as one of the best places to work. We could grow our own company regardless. We could put ourselves in a position to spread our word in a more meaningful way, all while maintaining our core values.

Not all of my team members were cut out for the game plan we established back then. In fact, we've since turned over our staff twice. These were all great people, but some of them were not willing to reset. Turnover is not always a bad thing. The Navy Seals' goal isn't to retain everyone; their goal is to put the absolute best people in the right positions and train them to handle anything. That's what I was determined to do with my team.

When I look back to the vision we outlined for eQ in 2009, I see that a good majority of those things have happened. My team is better, stronger, and more committed than ever. We've been recognized as among the best places to work in Baltimore. We've grown our business by 62 percent since 2009. In 2011, we recorded the best year we've ever had, even though the economy remains challenging. And you're talking to a guy who had never run a consulting company before 2001. We haven't accomplished a seismic level of earth-shattering success, but our story proves that the concept of growing regardless works. It really does. And it all begins with a proper reset.

Reset can have the same effect on your company—if you're serious about it. It's nothing but hard work. It's rolling up your sleeves, setting a new standard, and holding yourself and your team accountable to it. If you begin to negotiate on that standard, then frankly, that's not reset. That's nothing but a one-way ticket back to rehab.

The Philosophy

I usually try to avoid making assumptions, but I'm going to go out on a limb and make a couple of them here. I think it's safe to assume that every time you've read an advice book, attended a seminar, or made a New Year's resolution with the goal of improving some aspect of your life or work, one burning question has usually cropped up immediately: *How do I start?* You don't have the slightest idea, so you make a thousand excuses for why you can't move forward. Then you ask yourself another question: *Why isn't change happening?* The *need* for change is there. The *intention* to change is there. The *knowledge* necessary to make the change may even be there. But still, change doesn't occur.

That's happened to you at least once, twice . . . or thirty times, hasn't it? Let me assure you that you're not alone. The vast majority of people and organizations find it difficult to change, even when they really want to. In fact, in his book *A Sense of Urgency*, John Kotter writes that *70 percent* of organizational change initiatives fail. The failure rate is so high not because people are unwilling to commit to change, but because they are unwilling to un-commit . . . to their need to be right, or to past commitments they once thought were musts. They're not willing to go all in and put it all on the table. *They don't understand that they have the ability to hit the reset button and begin anew.*

 In his book *A Sense of Urgency*, John Kotter writes that *70 percent* of organizational change initiatives fail.

In my experience, reset is the most powerful way to think about moving forward, refocusing on a higher purpose, reclaiming your *why*, and living a story that serves you, your team, your company, and your community. When Kotter says that 70 percent of change initiatives fail, it's because the people involved didn't properly execute a reset. Reset done right leads to a zero percent failure rate.

So, what precisely is reset? Reset is what you do to start a new chapter. It's the willingness to lay it all on the line and to do so with eagerness and enthusiasm . . . not fear or reluctance. Ralph Waldo Emerson wrote, "Enthusiasm is the mother of effort, and without it nothing great was ever achieved." To reset means to surrender and become vulnerable; to develop a case of amnesia about the past and any previously limiting beliefs; and to move forward into a new world order. You state in word and deed that you will not be dragged down by a past that no longer serves you. You declare a new set of terms for the path forward, terms that, ideally, connect directly to your company's story and to keeping your word.

Steve Lishansky, my mentor, puts it this way: Reset applies to three different levels of leadership. It applies to you as a person. It applies to you as part of a team. And it applies to you as it relates to your company.

> Reset applies to three different levels of leadership. It applies to you as a person. It applies to you as part of a team. And it applies to you as it relates to your company.

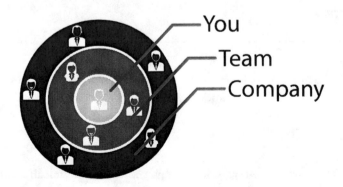

You

Team

Company

To launch a reset, you first have to go through the process as an individual. You must be willing to make tough decisions and put yourself in a position to grow regardless. There can be no sacred cows in your personal barn. Your willingness to reset must be based on more than self-interest. It must be centered upon what's best for your team, your company, your customers and your community. The same thing goes for your team. You've got to find common ground and gain agreement. You've got to find a way, again, to stay on point, stay on the mission, and stay consistent with your story as a team. Finally, you expand these concepts to your entire company.

Reset is about making a new verbal agreement with your people, your customers, and your community. It's a declaration that *we're all in this together . . . let's help each other get there.* One way to make that declaration in a meaningful way is to help those who are less fortunate. Volunteering as a team gives your constituents a fresh perspective about your organization. At entreQuest, we have "give-back days" in which we take on a community project and work together to create a positive impact. Instead of a typical quarterly retreat, we'll have a day of serving the homeless, or painting a school, or cleaning up a park—and *then* have our retreat. The result? A reset team . . . one that is more centered, more focused and more cohesive.

In October 2008, Starbucks president and CEO Howard Shultz exemplified this kind of reset. He had just returned to the Starbucks helm after being out of the picture for eight years. The economic downturn was in full swing, and the company was reeling. Sales were plummeting. Management made the gut-wrenching decision to close 600 stores and lay off scores of workers. And what did Schultz do in the midst of this crisis?

He took more than 10,000 of his managers and other employees to New Orleans to volunteer in the Hurricane Katrina rebuilding effort. How's *that* for redirecting focus?

As he painted a house belonging to a needy family in a neighborhood hit hard by the disaster, Schultz told reporters that given the tough economic times, he felt it was important for him and his company to reach out to their communities. But it was not all about altruism; it was also good business.

"Customers have many choices to make about all different types of products and services and a company that they trust, a company that has like-minded values to their own, is usually a company that they're going to support," he said.[8]

This reset in Starbucks' philosophy and strategy provided a new platform for conversation and for growth. Reset like that doesn't happen overnight, but the other steps in the growth methodology can't follow without it.

> Ralph Waldo Emerson wrote, "Enthusiasm is the mother of effort, and without it nothing great was ever achieved."

Reset is about letting go of all that's happened before—not forgetting it, but letting it go. There's a big difference. Forgetting means that you won't remember *anything*, including the valuable lessons you have learned. Letting go means that you'll remember the lessons, but you're going to drop the old ways of thinking and the emotional baggage that have damaged your company or caused pain, suffering and discontent.

According to Deepak Chopra, stress is the distance between where you are and where you want to be. Reset allows you to step back, understand the gap between those two places and assemble the right mindset and resources to close it. But beware! Often it's the gap that trips people up. It's not that they don't know how to close the gap, but they don't know how to let go of the things that prevent them from achieving such a closing.

One person who got reset right was Alan Mulally, CEO of Ford Motor Company. In 2008, while his cross-town neighbors GM and Chrysler were accepting a government bailout to rescue their companies in the wake of the economic downturn, Mulally took a different approach. The plucky CEO picked up a phone to call and thank customers who chose to buy a Ford over other cars. Michael Snapper of Grand Rapids, Michigan, received such a call. Snapper had already ordered a Toyota Prius, but when he saw Ford

8   Becky Bohrer, "Starbucks Helps Beautify New Orleans," *Seattle Post-Intelligencer*, 27 Oct. 2008, accessed 13 Oct. 2011, www.seattlepi.com/business/article/Starbucks-helps-beautify-New-Orleans-1289583.php.

trying so hard to stay afloat without accepting a bailout, he decided to take a closer look at its environmentally-friendly car. Snapper was so impressed that he cancelled the Prius and ordered a Ford Fusion Hybrid instead. He was shocked when Mulally called to thank him for choosing Ford.

After receiving Mulally's call, Snapper told a Grand Rapids television station, "We just decided, hey, let's buy an American car. Ford's doing its part and we can do ours too. [Ford] seems to me to *reflect a new attitude and a real commitment* to making their turnaround work" (emphasis added).[9]

In the end, Ford did not have to use any government money on its road to recovery. Instead, it reset its attitude and its way of doing business, and then instituted a holistic cost-cutting and restructuring effort that made it a better, faster, and stronger company.

Yes, this is a lot of work. No, the odds of success are not high. But you can do it if you approach reset logically and with firm resolve.

 The day you make your word the bond of yourself, your team and your entire organization, that's the beginning of reset.

The Process

If you accept this book's premise that everything in business is about relationships, then you also accept that there could come a moment in which a client or an employee feels that you haven't kept your word. You didn't live your story. You didn't give them the experience they thought they should get. Whenever that happens, you're going to carry around that discontent—that pain and suffering and resentment—and it's going to stunt your growth. It's going to be the antithesis of what **The eQ Growth Methodology** is trying to create.

To get past that, you must reset the relationship by following these steps, as laid out in the acronym RESET:

---

9   Lindsay Ropp, "Ford CEO Personally Thanks GR Buyer," WOOD TV, 3 Feb. 2009, accessed 7 Dec. 2011, http://www.woodtv.com/dpp/news/Ford_CEO_personally_thanks_GR_buyer.

- **R**ecognize: Awareness is everything. You have to be willing to find it. What you focus on, you will find.
- **E**xpose the elephant: Be willing to get to the core issue. Have candid conversations. Shine a light on the elephant in the room.
- **S**urrender: Be vulnerable. Accept, acknowledge, and apologize. Take full responsibility for the moment.
- **E**mpathize: Make sure the other person feels validated and valued.
- **T**erms and Time Frame: Establish the new world order and a time frame for achieving it.

The first step in the process is to **RECOGNIZE** that a reset is necessary. You've got to be aware when you're out of integrity with your word. I know that's a strong statement for some people, and I can hear the dissension all the way up here in Baltimore. *What do you mean "out of integrity with my word"? I'm doing exactly what I said I was going to do!*

Okay. I'll accept that. You're doing exactly what you said you were going to do. But are you doing what people *understood* you were going to do? That's the operative question. On an ongoing basis, are you providing an experience that is consistent with the promise you made, as they see it? Are you certain it hasn't changed even an inch? Because if it has changed even an inch in the eye of the beholder, then you are out of integrity with your word.

This means that reset could be happening in your camp on a daily basis, and, frankly, it *should* be happening on a daily basis. You should always assume you've messed up. You should always assume you're working at a deficit. You must never come into a conversation arrogant, overconfident, or even satisfied. Think back to the way the best teams play football: They play every minute as if it's fourth down and they're two touchdowns behind. Until that game is over, they don't let up. And because business is a game of relationships, it's never going to be over for your team, either. Because the second you take your eye off the ball, that's the second you're taking something for granted. Like the law of familiarity says: That which I know well, I will begin to take for granted. You have to be aware enough to recognize when you've taken someone for granted, so you can reset that relationship.

To recognize these dynamics, you need sufficient social awareness so that if someone is not feeling positive about the relationship or the experience they have had, you're able to diagnose it. The second step is that you must be willing to **EXPOSE** it. Be prepared to uncover the real issues and have candid conversations about what is actually at the heart of the matter. An employee survey is one way to expose the real issues in your company, but it doesn't always have to be that formal. You simply have to be willing to ask the tough questions, questions whose answers may make you feel uncomfortable. *How am I doing? Should I be doing more? What have I messed up? What's the real issue? Tell me more.*

This isn't about solving the problem . . . yet. This is only about having the guts to ask the questions and listen to the answers. Exposure is something you do throughout all the relationships in your organizational chain. It's about leadership talking to management, talking to frontline people talking to clients.

Let's assume you recognize the need for a reset and are willing to expose the problem by asking the tough questions. The next step is the hardest of them all: **SURRENDER**. It's time to own it. It's time to accept responsibility and to be honorable. It's time to be wrong. Most people aren't willing to be wrong. They don't want to own the issue because they think that if they own it, they will be vulnerable to an attack. But here's the secret: When you own up and accept responsibility for something, *you actually gain power.*

A former employee of mine once worked at the US Naval Academy. He told me about a tradition in which all the plebes are called out to the yard, ordered to drop for pushups, and then asked a question: *What is the definition of responsibility?* Most of the kids shouted out answers like ownership, owning the outcome, being accountable, accepting the blame. All of those were the wrong answers, and the plebes had to keep doing pushups until someone got it right. Eventually one of them shouted, "Taking responsibility is your ability to respond!"

That's the definition of responsibility: response-ability means to have the ability, the power, to respond.

That's the definition of responsibility: response-ability means to have the ability, the power, to respond.

If you own the responsibility, you will always own the ability to respond. When you blame the finance department because they didn't send the invoice correctly, or blame a delivery snafu on the new manager, or blame declining revenues on the sour economy, you're giving up your power to respond. The second you relinquish ownership is the second you lose the ability to do anything about it. You're just another victim.

The next E in RESET is for **EMPATHY**. Let's assume you recognized, listened, exposed the core issue, and took ownership. This is the time for making the other person feel valued and understood. Remember the Native American talking stick tradition in which the person holding the stick doesn't pass it on until they believe they've been heard? This is where you put that into practice. You stop, focus, and make sure the other person knows you have absorbed and accepted his or her position. You have to wait for that, even if you already have a response on the tip of your tongue. This cannot be contrived. In your heart, you must be empathetic to the other person's point of view. This is your chance to fill yourself with gratitude and perspective, to obtain a longer view and a higher level of sight.

This step reminds me of a client we once had that operated in the real estate market. In 2007, this company felt the early tremors of the impending crash. My team and I were tasked with helping them restructure their organization. With more than 400 employees, their leadership decided to cut staff by almost 70 percent. Generally, what companies do when they ax a bunch of people is they inconvenience the ones who remain by asking them to fly in so they can deliver the news. Or they'll have employees get on a webinar or a one-sided conference call in which they can't ask any questions. Leadership will deliver the news in fifteen minutes without giving folks a chance to digest it.

That's actually considered best practice, by the way. Bring people in, do the call, make sure everyone hears the news immediately. The leadership won't recognize or expose the real issues in this process, and they certainly won't be empathetic.

But in the case of this real estate client, we recommended that the top two executives, the CFO and the COO, get on planes and go visit the remaining sales teams in person. I went along with them. We visited fifteen cities in three days. We made ourselves available to the employees who were left. We sat with them and told them that we recognized this was going to be hard. We had candid conversations that exposed the real issues behind the layoff, and we talked about what was going to happen as a result. We called these "trash bag meetings." We went to each office, opened up the figurative trash bag, and allowed the staff to verbally throw up in it, one by one. People need to talk about traumatic changes, and we surrendered to that reality. Instead of saying the layoffs weren't their fault and blaming everything on the economy, the executives admitted the layoffs were the result of poor planning.

After allowing the staff to grieve for about a month, the initial shock wore off and we brought the team back into headquarters. At that point, we were able to reset the organization. In this case, that meant leadership not only provided the necessary empathy, but also brought the team on board with what we intended to do going forward. Over the next three years, this company went from bringing in around $20 million to almost $50 million per year. The empathy step was critical to their successful reset.

Assuming you can get past this step—assuming some trust remains—it's time to start talking about a new world order, otherwise known as new **TERMS AND TIME FRAMES**. Meaning, what is the new way we're going to operate together from now on? The new terms don't have to be entirely different from the old story or promise. It could be simply a new way of positioning the relationship. Or it could be you saying the same story or making the same promise, but with more intent and more empathy. Or it could be that the recipient actually believes in the terms this time around. That's all it takes.

People don't listen only to what we say. They also listen to what we do. Sometimes when we say something once, we assume the word has been spread and people will follow. Maybe that's true, but when was the last time you really absorbed something the first time around? When people don't know critical information or they don't remember it, they often make up their own rules. That's why spelling out the new terms and the time frame for how you're going to operate is so critical.

 People don't listen only to what we say. They also listen to what we do.

In this context, the "terms" are typically not legal terms or transactional viewpoints. Instead, they are important principles, values, behaviors, goals, purposes and time frames. Think of a weight loss analogy. If I say I want to lose a pound a month for the next 12 months, the number of pounds and the time frame in which I intend to lose them are critical components of the promise I make to myself. How can I keep myself on track and measure my progress if there are no terms and time frame attached to my goal?

President Bill Clinton, whether you like the man or not, is a master at framing. Appearing on an episode of *The Daily Show with Jon Stewart*, in seven minutes he explained better than anyone I've ever heard why the world is still in a financial crisis. What Clinton said was this: If you were to study any meltdown, recession, or depression that had anything to do with the real estate market in the last 500 years, you would see that the current crisis should take five to ten years to escape. But people aren't talking about five to ten years of being in this 1 to 2 percent growth phase. What people are talking about is recovery back to the life we knew in 2006, which is an inaccurate time frame. People haven't recalibrated their thinking on what "normal" should be.

Let's revisit the real estate company that laid-off seventy percent of its workforce. That company made painful changes and had to establish new terms. We helped them realize that on the relationship scale, they were starting at a negative three versus a positive three. Therefore, it was going to take longer to reach the positive three, four, or five they desired. When the economy tanked, our country lost $3 trillion to $4 trillion in wealth. We installed an $800 billion floor with the federal bailout. That means there's still a lot of climbing out to do. Had we been able to install a $4 trillion floor, our time frame for getting where we want to be would be shorter. Similarly, if I have over-leveraged my relationships, it will take longer to reset and establish a high-value connection with my clients and my people. It will take time, discipline, and a renewed dedication to personal responsibility to pull that off.

Speaking of these qualities, think back to the example of Ford Motor Company and its CEO, Alan Mulally. Mulally's empathy for Ford's constituents, while establishing a tough new set of terms and a rigorous time frame for moving forward, was stunning. You can't argue with the way Ford has reinvented itself, in essence creating a whole different model. Ford is a superb example of reset in many ways, most notably because it is a company that has been around for a century. If you've been thinking that the only way to achieve this growth methodology is to start your company from day one under these terms, think again. Look at Ford. To see an established company like that—an entrenched American institution—reset itself and come back from the abyss ought to inspire any business to give it an honest try.

Reset is hard, and reset takes time. In this context, reset reminds me of Chinese bamboo. Plant a bamboo sprout in the ground, and nothing happens for four or five years. You water and fertilize, water and fertilize, water and fertilize, but there is no sign that anything is happening. Then around Year Five, the bamboo tree begins to grow . . . and grow . . . and grow . . . *to a staggering ninety feet tall in just six weeks!* It seems incredible that a plant lying dormant for so long can suddenly explode with growth, but that's what happens. People speak in awestruck tones about the bamboo plant growing ninety feet in six weeks. In reality, it grew ninety feet in *five* years; you just couldn't see all the growth that was happening beneath the surface. The same is true for organizations that are resetting their philosophies and cultures. They are tending the unseen roots necessary for visible growth in the future.

You might be thinking, *Wow, this is going to take five years?* It could. Figuratively speaking, though, if in five years your company had ninety-foot relationships with your employees and customers, how bad would that be? This is not a how-to-fix-my-company-in-ninety-days proposition. But it's also not a how-to-fix-my-company-in-ten-years proposition, either. This method can make a meaningful, noticeable difference in your company in six to twelve months.

---

5 MUST-Ask Questions to Move
Your Culture to Be Growth Oriented

1. What really matters (the starting point for everything)?
2. What are we aiming for (gives you the direction to move forward)?
3. Why (gives you the inspiration to move forward)?
4. What is most important (gives you the focus to move forward)?
5. Who else cares (drives the shared energy to accomplish your goals)?

Reset in Practice: Doug Beigel and COLA

Doug Beigel oversees COLA, a physician-directed organization that promotes excellence in laboratory medicine and patient care through a program of voluntary education, consultation, and accreditation. COLA has accredited almost 8,000 medical labs, enabling them to meet federal and other regulatory requirements. To maintain COLA's vitality within a rapidly changing industry, Doug has had to constantly readjust and reset his organization.

Joe: I don't think I know anybody who's done the reset like you have, meaning having the willingness to put everything—including yourself—on the table; the willingness to be that vulnerable, especially

since you've done it multiple times. Why don't you give us some background?

Doug: I came to COLA twenty years ago, not necessarily looking to work in a not-for-profit organization. When I worked in non-profits before, I found that they didn't always live their mission every day. It's part of my DNA that if you are going to commit to something, your actions must follow your words. So, twenty-some years ago now, I was looking for an organization that was completely committed to meeting its stated objectives. It was a matter of finding a place that was interested in rationally living whatever it was they said they were going to do, and then doing it.

When I came to COLA, I met these visionaries—people who had an idea of something much bigger than themselves, and that was to improve laboratory medicine and patient care. In reality, it turns out they *were* so much bigger than themselves because when they created their mission, they didn't understand how to execute it. It was just their vision. Their spirit was tied to that. It was clear to them. In my interview, I asked them what would happen if they failed to meet their mission, and they said that failure was not an option.

That was what drew me to COLA in the first place. It was a start-up company that had very few resources. Certainly it wasn't the pay that hooked me, but the future promise. We took this tiny start-up and literally used the values of those original visionaries to cobble together an organization that not only wouldn't fail, but would actually meet its purpose. This is an organization with a sustainable mission. It wasn't just "climb this mountain and you're done." Improving patient care, participating in patient safety, really making a difference in the lives of patients—that was our *why*, and that would never change. But because of the dynamic environment in which we operate, how we live out our *why* and how we see ourselves in our relationships have to be very pliable to change.

Joe: One assumption people make is that reset is bad. Reset isn't rehab. You go to rehab when you're at rock bottom. At COLA, you went

about reset with an emphasis on the positive. I would love to hear more about that repurposing, that recommitting.

Doug: You're hitting on a differentiation that's really personal in some ways. As CEO, reset was the first step because you have to surrender to the fact that you're not always right, and you're probably not right in many ways. You have to be ready to aggressively go after what may be right. You have to see this as a continual experiment to continue trying to meet the mission.

The skills needed at start-up are much different than the skills I have developed and use today in my organization. At start-up, we were the smallest. We had no prior experience as an organization to do this. All the big players had created business models that would exclude the success of our organization because they would maintain control over the market. They had reputation. They had stature. They had been doing this work long before we arrived on the scene. That's another point at which I had to surrender to the reality.

We also had to learn how to look at the issues that were confronting me and the organization as opportunities, and not just as threats. I couldn't allow myself or the organization to feel victimized by that stuff. Literally, every situation became an opportunity to turn the industry on its heels.

We had no money to do what we were doing, but we decided to be the market leader in some critical issues. These were bold steps. You have to make sure you have a solid business model so that when you first recognize that something's not working, you can get out of it quickly. One of the other mindsets we've adopted is that change isn't bad. Not only is it not rehab, but also, if we're going to be the market leader or set a pace in this industry, then we have to have acquired competence in change. Even in our early years we said that the "C" in COLA stood for change.

The issue is in how do you deal with that. Fourteen years ago when we started talking about transformational change, the focus fell on the aspects of the organization that were bad. That was the initial conversation about transformation. We thought we were doing very well, thank you, until we entered an inquiry and could see the layers of how much better we could have been. We learned that the focus should not be on how bad we were, but how much better we could be.

Your market may have been doing things in a particular way for a hundred years, but what do the patients need *now* given the changes in technology? There are a whole bunch of things facing the American people when they try to seek healthcare today. How can we envision that, so that every time somebody goes into a laboratory, they're comforted by the fact that that laboratory is performing at peak? The idea is that we are responsible for that as though we were in that lab every day.

As a CEO, that's when you look at whom you have to work with, whom you have to convince to move forward. I wish you could snap your fingers and it would happen. But no, you have to convince . . . you have all these stakeholders out there and you have to persuade them. For example, I have a board that must have the same spirit as the original visionaries. Some come to our board already having that, and others need some convincing before they can become what we call COLA-teers. They need a little help understanding the world of possibilities lying before us.

Then we have all the people who work in our laboratories, and we have to convince them that this is a good thing we're doing. We're not there to put more stress in their lives. No, we're actually there in partnership with them. This isn't an example of, "We're the IRS and we're here to help." That's actually our anti-model. Our model is that we're all in this together.

Then we come to the patients. We want them enrolled in this so they understand the choices they're making when they elect to go to a lab that's not COLA-accredited.

And certainly then, our biggest stakeholder is the Centers for Medicare & Medicaid Services because they give us the license to operate. We can choose to see them as the mean government or we can enroll them into the process. We're electing to enroll them. They're our customer. It's not about "we-they." It's about "we" forming community and moving forward.

Then you throw price considerations into the mix, because you know you can't charge a gazillion dollars to a small doc's office or a healthcare clinic in the middle of nowhere. This market is price-sensitive, so we keep our prices low and we offer tremendous value for what they pay, value they can't get anyplace else.

I know that's a mouthful. You have to keep a lot of balls in the air, but if you're propelled by the vision of what your organization aspires to be and then just keep checking in on how you're doing, you'll move forward.

Joe: You have had to face both business and cultural challenges. How do you deal with that from a CEO's perspective?

Doug: This reminds me of the phenomenon that occurs whenever I tell people I work in a non-profit versus a for-profit organization, and all of a sudden it becomes a different conversation. I say it shouldn't be a different conversation. I think the role of every CEO is to capture that spirit in their workforce. I don't care if it's a multi-billion-dollar company or your church basement not-for-profit—the role is the same.

My premise is that every CEO has to inspire people and communicate why they're all there. What does the mission mean? It's up to the CEO to build that picture. You can see it when companies don't do that. Things other than mission fulfillment start to happen. To answer your question about how and why to do it, to me it is not Pollyanna-ish to say that the most important asset in a company is its people. CEOs can elect either to mobilize their people power for the good, or they can just basically allow the business to move forward and not use that power. Even if you don't use that power, it still exists, and the power can then be in the negative. You might talk to people throughout the organization and hear stories like, "Oh yeah, we get together and we talk about the fact that this company doesn't really care about us." Boy, that's power, too, but it's all negative. Instead, wouldn't it be great to have people gather around the water cooler and talk about how they can make things better for themselves and for the people we serve? That's not easy, and it's not for the weak-of-heart.

We had the tremendous opportunity to have Sylvia Smith Johnson, CEO of Maryland General Hospital, talk to us about her coming into a situation that was pretty bad. This is a hospital right in the heart of Baltimore City, a hospital with a wonderful mission of caring for the community's indigent people. But guess what? Employees didn't want to go to work every day at the hospital because they felt that nobody cared. Nobody cared at that hospital. But Sylvia Smith Johnson turned it around. She knew the power of those folks and the power of reminding them of their mission every day.

Joe: If I remember correctly, she went to her people and asked, "What do you think?" She used a survey to give her employees a voice. It was more around the intention of what the survey signified, versus the outcome.

Doug: That's right. She would say that survey was one way of listening. Absolutely critical.

Joe: What's interesting about her reset was that people were wallowing in Negative Land, as we call it. They didn't come running to her door begging to tell her what they thought. But over time, it sounds like things have changed. She's done a couple of surveys now, and the response rate for the second one has doubled over the first. Clearly, more people feel comfortable giving their voice because they're becoming confident that something good will come from it. What does reset mean to you?

Doug: It means that as CEO, you see that there are opportunities out there with your team, with your employees, with how to better serve your customers. You take a snapshot of your situation by offering a survey or through talking to folks. As CEO, you should know all your resources and whether they're aligned with moving in the direction your organization needs to go. Wherever you see disconnects or gaps forming, that's where the opportunities for reset are.

The reset we're going through now is clear: enroll our team into a common purpose so folks understand why we're here, so that they're fully engaged to make a difference in the world through COLA. And so reset means vulnerability. It's saying, "Okay, we chose to do an independent, anonymous survey. Let it fly." But before that, we made a conscious decision that this wasn't just a flat survey. This is a survey that is actionable. This survey isn't an intellectual exercise. It is a tool which will drive us towards actions, reforms, and reset. We're undertaking the survey because we're going to do something with these results. And, we aggressively communicate that fact to the team from the outset.

Joe: People are candid in your survey. They talked about you. They talked about the board. They talked about other executives. Having the stomach to put that out there is a pretty big deal. Be careful what you ask people, because they just might tell you what they think.

Doug: One of the comments was "[The] board should fire the CEO." Look, you want to take it personally to some extent, but you don't want to be so engaged in it that you can't see the opportunity. It took me probably ten reads to actually see all the abundance in their responses. Like you said, people came to it and were open. Rather than have people hide or not participate and not tell you what's really happening on the shop floor or in their interactions with the customers, they said what they felt. Isn't that wonderful? As I read the responses, I remember thinking, *How can these folks be present with our customers if they're feeling this bad?* Then suddenly I could see all the wonderful opportunities presented to us by having this knowledge. You have to surrender to the idea that any input is good input. That's pretty hard to do.

The next step was enrolling the leadership team. We've had several false starts with that. The leadership team is not trained in this stuff. Talk about taking things personally! But they're really committed people. It's kind of a fun thing, actually. We have enrolled them in this journey with us and that was risky because some of them said, "This isn't what I signed up for." There were certain segments of our business that were hit harder than others. People, including some on the leadership team, doubted that we were actually going to implement things to change. They believed that this would be a malignancy that would just fester out there and that we wouldn't do anything with it. We had to enroll them if we wanted to get beyond that.

We had to train them to get ready to surrender to implementation, because implementation could mean anything. We really had no way of knowing.

I can just imagine other CEOs reading this and thinking, "Oh gosh, you're gutting the organization!" No, you are resetting. You are moving the organization from the negative side to the positive side. Not to get too weird about it, but it's an energy transfer from "Let's not do anything" to "No, we want our team to get aligned and move and have impact." It's not pretty. It's not about suddenly telling people to change moving from left to right. This is an intense process and a commitment to mission.

Since it became clear that our organizational communication was not where it needed to be, we made a commitment to becoming good at communication if not the best at it we could be.

We wanted to make sure that we were really, really good at building the new story. This isn't just a story of a little non-profit organization in Columbia, Maryland, where people are dissatisfied with their working conditions. No, this is an organization that is moving forward. It's a good organization made up of powerful people committed to a much larger purpose that goes beyond themselves; an organization that people will soon look at and say, "What a privilege to work with an organization that can impact as many patients' lives in so many positive ways." We want to paint that future picture.

Part of our reset was to get involved with community efforts. People in this industry segment are not always seen as necessary valued members of the medical team, and they are. Seventy percent of medical decisions are based on quality laboratory results. We started videotaping some of our team members telling their personal stories to inspire people about who we are and what our mission is and what our impact is.

We also took the opportunity to say, "This was the satisfaction survey. You guys all read it. Great! Now that we're all inspired by the mission, let's go make changes." Everybody in the organization formed up in ten teams with one leadership team member on each. Their job was to pick from a list of issues that were of greatest concern to people on the employee satisfaction surveys and come up with a way to remedy that—but it had to tie back to the mission. Some people doubted that any of the recommendations would ever be approved, but others were starting to get inspired by the opportunity to have an impact.

Actually, some of the groups were ready to have an impact whether their efforts were formally approved or not. Approval meant that it eventually came to the CEO's desk for review. There were ten groups that worked for ninety days.

Joe: What kinds of issues were they considering?

Doug: Employee evaluations. Flexible work weeks. Four-day work weeks. Even the titles of our projects were opportunities for these teams to actually massage, change, impact our culture. We had teams that were cross-sections of every part of this organization trying to discover what it was they could change. No longer were they a single voice making a comment in an employee satisfaction survey. Now they were part of a change agent group tasked with understanding what the comments meant and bringing them to life in a way that improved our ability to meet mission. Even the initial naysayers couldn't stand on the sidelines too long because their peers expected them to complete work product and present it to the group. Pretty powerful stuff. Ultimately, I approved the recommendations made by each group which offered one.

What we've done is open up the opportunity for these groups to actually participate as advisors and maybe participate in implementation. I met with the employee performance group yesterday and asked them if they'd be interested in helping implement the projects. They said, "Oh yeah, absolutely. As a matter of fact, we're going to train to do it." It wasn't like they were asking permission about this. They were jumping at it because they felt invested in it.

Joe: What are some of the benefits you've seen from this process? And what are some things to watch out for?

Doug: I'll start with a "watch out." Don't go down this path unless you're ready to fully commit. If you come to the approval process with the mindset that you're going to approve no matter what the quality of the outcomes, you'll raise expectations and reinforce the negative stories that existed in the organization at the time of the survey. You have to be ready to judge them based upon how they fit tactically into the organizational mission. I made a decision early on that we needed a secret sauce to ignite our teams' passion for our mission. We needed a long-term commitment to amplifying their voices. If you assume your employees have no value and this thing is kind of weird, don't even go down this path. Those people have tremendous value. They interact with your customers every day. Capture their voice, capture their passion, do something about it.

Now to the benefits. I believe that it's untapped energy if you don't do anything with your people power. We've had people work weekends. We've had teams work into the night. Some of these are hourly employees, some of them are professional employees, but they've done their own research. This is not directed by management in any way beyond what it is they're working with. It's kind of like having an asset that has always been underutilized and now you're capitalizing on it. Once you ignite it, you're going to get at least twice the value, but there are areas in which you're going to get ten to twenty times the value.

For example, I gave this employee performance appraisal group ninety days to throw out the old process and bring in a new one based on creative, state-of-the-art approaches. The typical mindset would be throwing $50,000 to $100,000 at bringing in a consultant, someone who has to learn the culture from the ground up, and they're only going to recast something they already have lying around and probably not hit half of the issues our employees have with the existing process.

This is hard work. It's a journey. But I'd rather have this journey than try to force something on our people, something created by a consultant who doesn't understand this organization. Calculate the cost of the consultant. Calculate the man-hours to train up, and then look at the return on investment. My sense is I'd rather go this way. This way is pretty darn cool. It doesn't mean we're not going to bring in consultants at implementation, but it will be at one-twentieth of the cost.

From a business standpoint, our employees are our biggest asset. There's no doubt about it. By engaging them in this way, we're beginning to get a glimpse of what's going to happen in this organization as we work to meet mission. Then there are the long-term cultural benefits. When I think about culture in organizations, most CEOs I meet are pretty jaded about looking at the past three years. You couldn't have forecast that. My position has always been that as CEO, it is my responsibility to make sure that you're ready for any changes that might come up. Mission probably shouldn't change much, but just about everything else can and will.

We're building a forward-looking community that will embrace the changes and future transformations in a way that will make us better, so that we can more effectively serve the laboratories and their patients. On a micro level, there's a lot of respect among everyone in the organization no matter what they do. If they're in the mail room, at the office processing paperwork from the laboratories, or if they're actually surveyors in the field or part of government relations, whatever their role, there is a binding appreciation that's now starting to form. It's not this "we-they" anymore. It's a "we" conversation now. It's potent. The other part of it is that whereas most organizations have silos, we're giving people freedom to move around in the organization to discover what they can do to help. It's not about territoriality. It's not about exclusion. It's about inclusion for the right purposes, and to me that's a secret sauce. Some quick hits about reset are that you're going to have naysayers, without a doubt. Another quick hit would be to take every opportunity to reinforce mission. Stay on message. If you do, within a matter of days you'll start seeing a change in the conversation. The organization won't be conscious of it, but you'll see it as the CEO.

For instance, we had a conversation around four-day work weeks. The gist of the first conversation I heard was, "We can't go to the four-day work week because we have customers out there five days a week." And someone piped up and asked if flexible time might be helpful. So the group started looking at it as not just about a four-day work week, but how we can be flexible in the way we treat folks. They started to see that we had an opportunity. We have customers on the West Coast and all of a sudden the idea arose that maybe some people could come in at 10 o'clock or 11 o'clock in the morning to better serve them. Soon, the conversation turned to the opportunity to have virtual employees.

What started out as, "Gee, I wish I could work four days instead of five" as part of an employee satisfaction survey turned into a robust conversation that propelled this team. They even did surveys on their own. They talked to their peers. They talked to people in different parts of the company. They came out with something that frankly is much more robust than what we ever imagined.

And here's another quick hit: Nine out of ten employee initiatives were approved. Now why is that a quick hit? Because trust is such a major issue in any organization. People want to be listened to. Take Sylvia Smith Johnson—her people wanted to be listened to. People want their voice to have meaning. That is why you don't go into this with a sense that you're only going to go halfway. If you're going to raise the questions and people are going to provide the answers, then it's incumbent upon you to implement. Because if not, that's a hit that you don't want to take.

Joe: Well, that's the status quo, right? Ask questions, listen, do nothing about it.

Doug: Right.

Joe: The other piece about the nine out of ten initiatives, beyond the building of trust, is this: When's the last time any organization has moved the needle on nine core initiatives during the course of normal business? I think that is huge. Even if the things aren't entirely new concepts, the fact that you're going to execute them is major.

Doug: Yes, the early decision was if we're going to do this, we've got to do it all the way. Understand how to do this right, and have the attitude that it will succeed no matter what comes up. There are going to be a lot of things come up that will feel harmful on their face, but those are opportunities to actually move the organization forward.

Listen to the people; spend time exploring concepts with folks. People maybe have perceived you not being present before. Well, now you *are* present. Grab that low-hanging fruit. It's just tremendously powerful when you do that.

You have to remember that reset is a journey. It's multi-dimensional. There really isn't an end to it. It's just one opportunity after another to move forward toward the mission. People learn from those progressions, but as a CEO, I think it's important to understand how the evolution is happening. It could be that you select the employee team process and you have ten teams that have a beginning, middle, and end to them, but then you have implementation that takes it further. This is really about resetting an organization in perpetuity. Reset, reset, reset. Even though we're at the end of some of the employee groups and I'm in the approval process, my role is to encourage them to continue participating. It's up to me to remind them that this is a journey and we need to keep focused on our customers.

There are so many opportunities to be better at what we do. My job is just to continue to listen, continue to show people how committed we are to them and to our mission, and then create ways to keep everyone moving forward.

Exercise: Planting the Seeds for Growth through Reset

Resetting yourself can be the most challenging, but it may be the step that needs to happen the most. Resetting with yourself requires you to be brutally honest about how you are feeling about what's happening in your company, why you feel that way, and what you can do about it. To reset yourself, use as a starting point our exercise on "25 Reasons Why" described in Chapter 5.

Next, think about your habits relative to having candid conversations with employees or clients and dealing with conflict. What are these habits? How will they show up when you try to reset with these constituents? How do you plan to overcome them? The following table provides a framework for thinking through a reset in terms of yourself, your manager, your direct reports, other team members, and the company as a whole. Now, RESET! Remember to be thoughtful and compassionate.

RESET Summary	Action Items	You	Your manager	Your direct reports	Other team members	Whole company
R = recognize or discover what you and others are thinking	Determine if a RESET needs to happen with you, your manager, your direct reports, other team members, or the entire company.					
E = expose the real issue	Determine the real issue and your plan for bringing it to the constituent's attention.					
S = surrender, accept responsibility	How can you accept responsibility for the real issue? What could you have done differently or more of?					
E = empathy, make the other person feel valued or understood	What will be your biggest obstacles to conveying empathy? What's your plan for making this constituent feel understood and valued?					

RESET Summary	Action Items	You	Your manager	Your direct reports	Other team members	Whole company
T = terms and time frames for moving forward	What are you aiming for relative to shared principles, behaviors, goals, whys, purposes, and time frames? What are you willing to agree to?					

Additional Resources

For more ways to plant the seeds for growth through Reset, visit www. growregardless.com/book/reset for a free training video.

Chapter 5

STORY—START
WITH WHY

People don't believe what you tell them.
They rarely believe what you show them.
They often believe what their friends tell them.
They always believe what they tell themselves.
What leaders do: they give people stories they can tell themselves.
Stories about the future and about change.
—Seth Godin

In the early 2000s, the high school graduation rate in inner-city Baltimore hovered close to a dismal twenty percent. A product of the city school system myself, I decided to join efforts with three other entrepreneurs to seek a solution to that problem. We thought there had to be a way to bring the private sector into the schools in a meaningful way, because although there are hundreds of great mentoring programs, there aren't many workplace-based programs that operate like a business model. We decided to create a vision that one day out of each month, every Baltimore City high school would be empty because all the kids would be spending the day in a corporate workplace, being mentored by a young professional and exposed to things they might not have access to otherwise.

We came up with a foundation called b4students—the "b" stood for Baltimore and for business—designed to increase graduation rates by linking high school kids with local businesses. To launch and sustain the foundation, we each pledged $25,000 a year for four years to cover our staff costs in executing the program; and we asked other companies to do the same. The idea was that when companies signed on to participate, their individual programs would be theirs to nurture and grow. We envisioned that each company would mentor kids for their entire high school experience. This long-term commitment was different from anything then available in youth mentoring, but we believed that's what it would take to make an enduring impact on these kids' lives.

We recognized that four years and $100,000 was a hefty commitment. To convince companies to come on board, we told them b4students was important for Baltimore and would make a significant difference in students' futures. We used my personal story of being a product of Baltimore City schools as a real-world illustration. I was a kid whose own senior class was decimated by a high dropout rate, yet I managed to overcome it with a little luck and some caring mentors of my own. But our message wasn't resonating. We kept hitting brick walls; not a single company would commit to join us. Eventually, we realized that just because my story was true didn't mean it would necessarily connect with everyone.

It wasn't that we had to make up a new story, but we realized we needed to tweak it with an eye toward our audience and what was most important to them. Although corporate philanthropy was important to the audience, what was really important to them was having a way to be philanthropic while simultaneously improving their employee experience. They wanted to improve their retention, profits, performance, culture, and turnover rates. They wanted to attract more qualified candidates and, at the same time, be part of a community of other private-sector companies giving back in a meaningful way.

So we revised our story to say that partnering with b4students would benefit not only the kids and the community, but also the participating companies. Becoming part of this project would make a difference in the lives of employees. It would increase morale, improve culture, and give the companies a terrific public relations boost. Our new and improved story made it okay to be selfish because the companies would be giving something of value in exchange for receiving something of value in return.

Almost immediately, we got our first "yes," and more soon followed. Since then, b4students has become a model program that has raised the city's graduation rate from approximately twenty percent to ninety percent among participating students; and it's now being proposed as a nationwide model for workplace-based mentoring programs.

One of the students involved with b4students gives us an even stronger example of the power of story. This young man told us that when he was growing up, he wanted to be a chef. Simply graduating high school would have been a major coup for this kid; becoming a professional chef would have been remarkable. To help him understand himself and his goal better, we took him through an exercise called "25 Reasons Why." We sat him down with a piece of paper and a pencil and told him to come up with twenty-five reasons why he wanted to be a professional chef. You can imagine what the first few reasons were.

"I want money," he said with a grin. "I want a car and new clothes and shoes, and jewelry and a big house and a vacation house by the beach. I want to travel and see the world and go to concerts. And I want lots and lots of ladies!"

The kid was having a ball . . . until we got to around the 10th reason. Then he stopped. He couldn't come up with any more reasons why becoming a chef was so important to him.

Suddenly, he blurted out, "Oh, here's another one—I love serving people! I didn't grow up with a lot of food, so feeding people makes me really happy."

"I love being creative and making something from nothing," he continued. "I love trying new things and giving people an experience they've never had. I love the fact that I would be setting a good example for my younger brothers and sisters."

Now the list was becoming more personal, more connected to a higher purpose. But the exercise is not called "25 Reasons Why" for nothing, so we pushed him to continue. He got stuck at eighteen, and it probably took half an hour before he thought of another reason. A few minutes later he got to twenty, then twenty-three. He begged us to let him stop, but we made him keep going. He slouched over the table, pounding it with his fists and groaning.

Suddenly, he sat up straight.

"All right, you know why I'm really doing this? I'm doing it because someone's got to thank our grandmother who raised me and my brothers and sisters," he said with conviction. "Someone's got to pay her back and thank her for all the sacrifices she's made. Someone's got to take care of her when she gets older, because she took care of us. It's going to be my job to take care of her."

Now that, my friends, is a story.

The Philosophy

There are two kinds of stories: those we tell others and those we tell ourselves. The story we tell others are what we believe to be true; it's either a story we've created based upon an experience we've had ("I stayed at a Kimpton Hotel and it was great") or something we read ("I saw an interesting article about how Kimpton values its employees"). Most of the time, we will believe what we read if our personal experience is reasonably close to it. When you tell people the story of how your company started, you create a fascination, a curiosity and a deeper connection between all the relationship links in your organizational chain. Then, if people's experiences consistently reinforce that story—if you keep your word—you will have forged a bond that is extremely difficult to break.

A good story isn't only about what a company has done in the past. It can also be about where the company is going in the future. It's like President John F. Kennedy saying in 1961 that America was going to put a man on the moon within ten years. What inspired us about that story was that it was audacious, it brought us together, it was competitive, it was exciting . . . and there was a definitive end point. It got us fired up. President

Kennedy got us dreaming about shooting for the stars, and he brought all of us along for the ride. He was so effective that a reporter once asked a janitor what he did at NASA, and he replied, "I'm helping to put a man on the moon!"

That's what a good story can do for your organization. A good story drives our beliefs. It helps us remember things. It causes us to think and act differently. A good story binds and connects us. Stories are the way we've always communicated; we used to sit around a campfire 3,000 years ago and tell stories to pass information from generation to generation. Stories have been essential to our development as a species.

You could say that a story is a rallying cry, an expression of a company's vision, a communication of its values, mission, purpose, brand . . . and you would be right. A story is all of those things. But it's even more than that. A story is a *promise* to your two most important assets: your employees and your customers. It's a promise of who you are and what folks are going to get by working with you or doing business with you.

A story is a *promise* to your two most important assets: your employees and your customers.

Here's what a story is not: It's not some fictitious bedtime tale. It's not something cute to hang up on the wall. It's real. It's a living, breathing expression of what your company once was, what it is now, and what it aspires to be in the future. You know you have a great story when your employees *know it, own it, and drive it.* Knowing it is intellectual. Owning it is emotional. Driving it is passion and will at work. When you have a story that strong, there is zero tolerance for not living it out and not keeping that promise.

Can companies do business without having a good story? Of course. They do it all the time. There are many reasons why companies don't tell their stories. Maybe their leadership is bashful. Maybe they haven't taken the time to think it through. Maybe they don't believe it's important. But it is. They're missing out on a golden opportunity to inspire others. Remember, we're all looking for meaning in our lives; we want to hear inspiring things. So when you have a great story, you increase the odds of growing regardless of your size, your current economy and your industry. The new-new reality we outlined in Chapter 2 makes a compelling story essential for growth.

Today, we're bombarded with more messaging than ever before. Our attention is diverted in a thousand directions. Information overload and rapid social change have left many of us craving meaning in our lives. A great story remedies all of that and elevates your company in the eyes of your people and your clients. That's why **The eQ Growth Methodology** begins with Story.

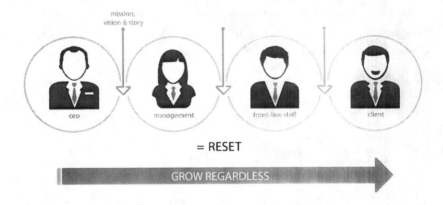

You can see that the story emanates from the leadership and flows throughout the chain to the client. Think of some of the most inspiring leaders of our time: Martin Luther King, Jr., Desmond Tutu, Mother Teresa, Winston Churchill, or, if you're a sports fan like me, Vince Lombardi. These people moved mountains in their respective fields because they were trustworthy, passionate, and real. They had a sense of urgency. They had strong convictions. They knew exactly why they were doing what they were doing, and they told us stories about that.

To see what I mean, watch Dr. King's "I Have a Dream" speech on YouTube. By the way, YouTube is one of the greatest tools we have at our disposal and it's free, so take advantage of it to learn more about great storytellers. Spend an afternoon watching other inspirational masters and studying how they do it. You're about to become a storyteller, too. You're going to be communicating your story to your people, your clients, and your community. Learn how to do it with passion and conviction, and you too will move mountains.

Let's say you have five hundred people in your organization. What if you and each of those people committed to telling your company's story to one new person a month for the next twelve months? What if you each committed to telling it to one new person *every day for a year?* Hearing an inspiring story about your organization, told by someone the listener knows and trusts . . . how much is that kind of advertising worth?

It's priceless, that's how much it's worth. And it doesn't cost you a dime.

The Process

It's funny. We have so many means of communication—the Internet, cell phones, web cams, and Blackberries, a host of cool technology designed to link us to one another—yet we have stopped telling each other stories. We're certainly not telling stories about what we do with the majority of our waking time, which is work. We're not talking about it because we're not excited about it. I understand that you can't just be excited for excitement's sake; you have to feel it. It has to be genuine and authentic, or it's a bunch of nonsense. The way to uncover that authenticity is to discover your "why." Why do you do what you do? Once you and your people know your individual *whys* and your collective *why*, you can all begin to tell your company's story with conviction.

Simon Sinek, author of *Start with Why*, has a wonderful explanation for how this works. Sinek studied why people like Martin Luther King, Jr. and companies like Apple were successful, and he discovered that they consistently think, act, and communicate in a way that is the exact opposite of most of us. He calls this manner of communication the Golden Circle: the *what* makes up the outermost part of the circle, then the *how*, and finally the *why* in the center. But doesn't the *why* drive the *what* and the *how*? That's why I like to think of the Golden Circle more as interlocking gears working off each other.

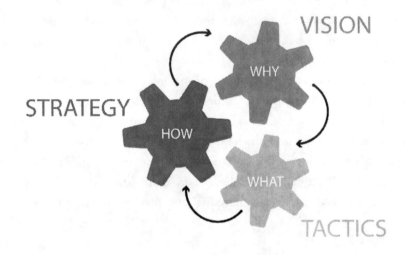

We all know "what" we do. My *what* is that I teach people to grow their businesses. My neighbor is a doctor who helps sick people. My dad runs a trucking company. That part is easy to define. When we tell others what we do, they typically nod and say, "Okay," and go on with their day, uninspired.

Next, we all know "how" we do what we do. I teach people to grow their businesses by conducting trainings and writing articles and books, among other things. My neighbor helps sick people by giving them medicine. My dad keeps the trucking company running by supervising workers and facilities. That's the process, and that's also fairly easy to explain. When we tell others *how* we do what we do, again they usually nod and say, "Okay," and go on about their business.

But according to Sinek, the center of the circle—the *why*—is the magic question. The answer to that question holds the key to telling our company story with conviction in a way that gains people's trust and loyalty. While we all know what we do and how we do it, we don't always know *why* we do it. It's easy to say we run our businesses to make money, but that's a result, not a driver. I understand that making money is a core element of business, but there must be something deeper. Uncover what that deeper thing is, tell people about it in a compelling manner, and you're on your way to making it happen. (Do this effectively, and you'll probably end up making more money, too.)

Why is your company here? Why do you do this work? Sinek found that the people and companies that most effectively communicate their *whys* are more likely to succeed and to get what they want. Those who communicate from the inside of the Golden Circle outward (who first articulate *why*, then *what*, and *how*) inspire more trust and loyalty than those who communicate from the outside in.

So when people communicate from the outside of the Golden Circle in, when they tell us *what* they do, we certainly can understand it. However, we probably won't act on that information. But when people or organizations convey a message about *why* they do what they do, we experience the kinds of feelings that influence our behavior. So if you want to get folks to do something for you, for your organization, or for themselves, you must appeal to that portion of the brain that orders action, and you do that by telling a story that starts with *why*.

Tell It Like It Is

There are many ways to tell a story effectively. One of my favorites is outlined in *The Hero's Journey*, by author and scholar Joseph Campbell. Campbell studied myths around the world and distilled them to their basic elements: order, chaos, and resolution.

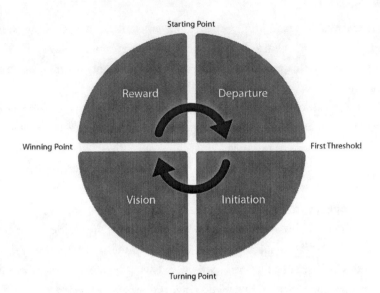

According to Campbell, most stories begin with all being right in the protagonist's world (order), until something happens to throw things out of kilter (chaos). After a series of trials and tribulations, things return to a relative state of normalcy (resolution). In the present day, most movies follow this progression. Take *Rocky*, for instance. The starting point is that Rocky was a bum. He had no money, no girlfriend, no job; he barely had a place to live. Rocky's chaos began when he got a call from the heavyweight champ, Apollo Creed, challenging him to a fight. Rocky had to make a decision: to fight or not to fight. He decided to fight. Resolution came when he knocked Apollo Creed down, the fight ended in a draw and he got the girl. Rocky's goal wasn't to win the championship; it was to stop being a bum. It was to stand up to the test in front of the whole world. He passed that test and got his resolution.

Rocky's story was a logical progression from order to chaos to resolution, which is why we all understood it. And his story was grounded by his *why*, which is why we all cared.

Examples of this are everywhere. Think of the Michelin tire ad: "So much is riding on your tires." That ad is not focused on the tire or what's important to Michelin; it's focused on you and *why* you need good tires.

Here are other examples of those kinds of stories:

- Wal-Mart: To give ordinary folks the chance to buy the same things as rich people.
- Nike: To experience the emotion of competition, winning. and crushing competitors.
- HP: To make technical contributions for the advancement and welfare of humanity.
- Coca-Cola: To put Coke within arm's reach.
- Harley-Davison: To fulfill dreams through the experience of motorcycling.
- Google: To not be Evil.

A good story answers two questions. Why should the customer care? Why does the company care? A story must be written down and communicated in a variety of ways throughout the company and throughout the community.

In the late 1800s, a sixteen-year-old boy left his family in Sweden and came to America, following the promise of a better life. He arrived with five bucks in his pocket, and he didn't speak English. He was all alone. It was the time of the great Gold Rush, so by working in mining and logging camps, the boy was able to make his way to Washington State and eventually to Alaska, where he bought a plot of land with the money he'd earned. Unbeknownst to him at the time, his land had millions of dollars' worth of gold on it. But a neighboring landowner and a corrupt local politician cheated the young man out of almost all of his money.

So what was his story about America now? Was it still the land of opportunity, or a place in which hardworking people get the shaft? This young man decided that America was still the land where dreams come true. He chose to go to Seattle, where he and a partner opened a shoe store. He didn't know a thing about shoes, but he worked hard and gave every customer an unconditional guarantee. This man grew his shoe company and eventually passed it on to his kids, who followed his example, grew the company and passed it onto their kids. Today it's a $9 billion business, one of the world's biggest apparel companies. It consistently wins awards for employee and customer service because it has retained its founder's dedication to hard work and fair play.

And who was that founder? John Nordstrom.

You've probably heard of Nordstrom, but this may be the first time you've heard their story. It's a tale that automatically draws you in. You can picture the struggling immigrant . . . the hard worker . . . unshakable integrity . . . a never-say-die mentality. It makes you feel like you know something about John Nordstrom, his family, and his company.

This concept hit home for me during my time repairing Stan Burns' mansion after my painting crew trashed it. Stan had taken up writing during his retirement, and he had been tapped to write the story of Enterprise Rent-A-Car.

Enterprise was started by Jack Crawford Taylor, a young man who barely made it through high school. Taylor dropped out of college and served as a fighter pilot in World War II before returning to St. Louis and going to work as a Cadillac salesman. He came up with the idea of running a rental car service and convinced his boss to set aside space for the fledgling company in the dealership's body shop.

Taylor took a fifty percent pay cut in exchange for a twenty-five percent share of the profits, and he named the company Enterprise in honor of the aircraft carrier on which he served during the war. He started with only seven cars. Even though his service was competing with giants like Avis and Hertz, Taylor found ways to give his customers excellent service, including locating his cars away from airports and closer to where people lived, and giving customers a ride to and from the Enterprise location. "We'll Pick You Up" became the company's catchphrase.

Today, Enterprise has more than 6,000 locations in the United States and abroad.

No discussion of corporate story would be complete without Starbucks, whose mission is "to inspire and nurture the human spirit—one person, one cup, and one neighborhood at a time."[10] Here are other elements of the Starbucks story, which could just as easily be called the Starbucks Promise:

- It's our goal for all of our coffee to be grown under the highest standards of quality, using ethical trading and responsible growing practices.
- Our stores are a welcoming third place for meeting friends and family, enjoying a quiet moment alone with a book, or simply finding a familiar place in a new city.
- We believe in treating our partners with respect and dignity. We are proud to offer two landmark programs for our partners: comprehensive health coverage for eligible full- and part-time partners and equity in the company in the form of stock options.
- We are committed to doing business responsibly and conducting ourselves in ways that earn the trust and respect of our customers, partners, and neighbors.

---

10   Mission Statement, Starbucks, accessed 8 Sept. 2012, http://www.starbucks.com/about-us/company-information/mission-statement.

> • It's our goal that by 2015, all of our coffee will be grown using ethical trading and responsible growing practices; one hundred percent of our cups will be reusable or recyclable; we plan to contribute one million volunteer hours each year to our communities.

As long as your experience with Starbucks supports what you've read here (that is, as long as Starbucks keeps its promises), you'll go back again and again. And if your experience there happens to be consistently remarkable, you'll tell their story to others, who will go check it out for themselves.

That's called growth. That's what a good story can do. And here's how you do it, step by step:

1. **Get clear on your *whys*.** As an executive team or as an owner, do the exercise "25 Reasons Why" and think about what it tells you. Why are you doing what you do? Why does your company exist? If you had to be certain about the values and drivers that are most important to you, what would they be?

2. **Get clear on how to assimilate your personal story to those *whys*.** Once you understand why your company is here, the next phase is assimilating your personal story: who you are, why you are unique, and what gifts you bring to this world. What was the significant emotional event that led you to your *why*? For example, Chapter 1 is about the significant events that led me to start my company and eventually write this book. Having a great entrepreneurial experience and outstanding mentors who helped me see that making money didn't have to be mutually exclusive with making a difference were significant turning points that led me to formulate my *whys*. What are yours?

3. **Figure out for whom you do business.** Who are your customers? What do they get when they do business with you? How does that help them fulfill *their* missions? How is that unique in the marketplace? Why is it important?

Story in Practice: David Zdrojewski, John Walden, and VibrAlign

VibrAlign, founded in 1983 and based in Richmond, Virginia, provides value-added, easy-to-use shaft alignment systems and vibration solutions to customers nationwide. It offers field services, training, and a range of laser alignment tools backed by superior customer service. Business partners David Zdrojewski and John Walden have woven their values and those of their company into a masterful story that motivates them and their employees, clients and community every day.

Joe: You both are seasoned entrepreneurs who have been very successful in business. You've been pragmatic financially, but innovative from a growth perspective. When you first heard about this concept of story for a company, what did you think it meant?

David: I thought it meant that maybe you were a little crazy. I'm a guy who's focused on P&L. I have been all my life. But after we started writing our story, I was surprised by how much sense it made. The real benefit in the story is that it uncovered all our core values. As a sales company, we've tried a lot of different sales techniques, but what's more compelling than a good story?

John: Having come from such a long sales career, the most interesting part about the story to me was the idea that if you're not telling your story, somebody else is telling your story. VibrAlign is in a niche market with very few competitors. We've allowed our competitors to tell our story because we didn't know any better, and over the years they've put us in some pretty bad lights. So the story became really important to me for that reason.

From a sales perspective, it clicked with me quickly because I realized that's exactly what I do, what I've done, and what I've asked our people to do is to learn about our products, our competitors, our marketplace and our customers, and then weave our story together so that the customer gets to the empathy feeling that needs to occur in order to make a sale. So it clicked with me quicker than it did for David, but that's the essence of it for me, is that *If you're not telling your story, then somebody else is.*

Joe: David, you talk about how this helped extract and make the values more explicit for you. Tell me more about that.

David: As you know, my eyes are on the profit all the time. As we were writing the story, I heard one of your people say something to the effect that the number one responsibility of the sales manager is people development. I think that when you focus on your people rather than the P&L, all of a sudden the story starts to make sense. So if my sales manager's job is people development, then it's got to be my job, too.

Joe: How was developing the story different than developing a vision or mission statement?

John: The exercise of developing the story forces you to truly look inside as the business owner and figure out what you want your company to be. Historically, we at VibrAlign have always viewed ourselves as a family. Every family has its issues, its problems. What the story did is solidify all the things that you would do in a family with young kids. You would look at your kids and you would think about the values that you want to be able to teach them: how to be passionate about things, how to love other people, how to be open, how to be focused on what they want. A lot of the core things that you see in our story are the same things that you want to be able to pass along from generation to generation.

Joe: There's certainly a process and a science to developing a story, but there's also an art, and you're beginning to hit on that art piece, John. As an owner, the story transcends your chosen business and illuminates your core, your personal views. It's not just about the company; it's about you two and what you believe.

David: That's right. You know, as much as I hate doing it, I'm a huge fan of the "25 Reasons Why" activity. I think it's really beneficial personally, and of course it was really helpful in developing the story. By the time we came to you for help, John and I had become so bogged down in thinking about all the stuff that we didn't like or want, but when you helped us put our story down on paper and we started thinking about what we'd like, what we want, we shifted our focus to where we're going instead of where we don't want to go. That was huge. It changed my whole mental outlook, to be honest with you.

John: I agree. I think this idea that you gave to us, to run toward what you want instead of running away from what you don't want, was a game changer. I've tried to figure out other ways to say that and I always come back to "Run toward what you want." That's what we've tried to do. And I think what it does for employees is to let them know, without even picking up a management by objectives plan or looking at their job description, what it is they're supposed to be working toward. They should have a feel, just from reading VibrAlign's story, of what the company is doing. One of the things David and I used to get complaints about all the time was that people didn't know where we were going, or they didn't know what we wanted.

David: Or that there was bad communication. We got that a lot.

John: So what this does is create an umbrella under which all of that communication can occur.

Joe: Why don't you both give me your experience in going through the "25 Reasons Why" exercise as it relates to putting together the VibrAlign story?

John: We're an engineering-based company and we sell an engineered product. It's always been easy for us to think in terms of *what* and the key for me in developing this story was understanding the importance of *why*.

David: Which seems to make the customers connect on a personal level.

John: Exactly, but the *why* is not only for our customers. It's also for our employees. When we looked at the "25 Reasons Why" as we were developing this story guide, they really came around to why we are even in business. What do we do this for?

David: That activity of doing the twenty-five *whys* was painful the first time and maybe even more painful the second time, but John and I are both—I wouldn't call us religious—but we are spiritual. We're both God-fearing. The thing that made us connect with the exercise is that when you get to those last few *whys*, I mean, that's higher purpose stuff. That's why it's easy to sink our teeth into it. The higher purpose stuff is important to us and it always has been, but going through the twenty-five *whys* helped us realize that, yeah, we're in business to make money and we want to grow, but there's also a higher purpose to all of this.

Joe: What have been some of the benefits of naming your *whys*?

David: We've had one of the best years we've ever had this past year, and I am certain that part of it had to do with us clarifying our values. Would you agree, John?

John: Yes, I think so, too.

David: I am so optimistic about next year, I can hardly stand it. I think we're on track to go through the ceiling. I really do. I've never been as optimistic about the business as I am right now. Never. We just had a very good year in a really tough economy. And for someone like me who really cares about the numbers, it's important to note that this hasn't cost us any dough. We didn't go backward at all.

John: We have a unique organization in that we have two guys sitting on top of it. That doesn't always work well, but David and I have worked well together for ten-plus years. We never really understood why we worked well together until we went through this activity.

David: Oh, that's so true.

John: As we were first working through the process, it was startling to see how many common things there were across our list of *whys*. Don't get me wrong, we disagree fairly often. But we are able to work those things through because we have these common *whys*, not because we look at things the same way. What the "25 Reasons Why" activity did was clarify for us why we work together so well.

David: Since starting this process, John and I are more real with each other than we've ever been. We've always worked well together, but we relate better now, and it's been really huge for us. It's not only in the story development aspect of this, but also in other things you've taught us. It's been almost like therapy. It helps us learn to relate and do better together.

John: I also know this: Since we put out the story guide for VibrAlign, I have noticed that the decisions being taken by my subordinates seem to be much better and more sound than they have been in the past.

Joe: When we first rolled this out to your company, what kinds of things were going through your minds? Any concerns?

John: I have one vivid memory of something that happened the evening after we met with our people about this for the first time. We finished the meeting, went out to dinner and returned to our hotel, and I got a call from a subordinate whom I've known for many years. We ended up having this emotional conversation, much of it about our company's *why*, and the call lasted for four hours. The only reason it didn't last longer was because the battery on my phone ran out. But rolling out the story concept to our people helped us connect, on an emotional level at least, with many of them.

David: I do think that as we started to roll this story out, there was some trepidation; perhaps some people thought we had lost our minds. This is the soft side of business, and you know the soft side doesn't sell all the time. This is when the difference gets made. Not everyone is comfortable right off the bat. But we have a video of our people telling our story, and when you see the video, it's clear that they were into it. They *are* into it. It's an awesome video. It's not slick and professional, but it's loaded with the emotion that John speaks about. It stirred up the passion in the organization. That's incredible. You can do a million things to try to stimulate the numbers and what have you, but what do passionate people do? How valuable is that?

John: Passionate people will climb mountains and forge streams for you.

Joe: As you've started to hit some of the daily routines of running a sales organization, how often does this story concept come up?

John: Quite a bit.

David: I would say, for me, almost every time.

John: We're still learning, especially at the interaction level with the client. We're still learning how to do this well. I still see some of our people stumbling with it but I see that—I hope I'm not looking through rose-colored glasses—I see that as more of an issue of being able to communicate as it is an issue of understanding. I think our people understand it. They are not real comfortable with communicating it yet. Probably ninety percent of this organization is technical-oriented and engineering-oriented. When you take an engineer and you tell him to do something that is . . .

David: . . . touchy-feely.

John: Yes, it takes a while to get comfortable with it. If you tell them, "This is a screw and it needs to go into this piece of wood and it needs to be attached at this place," they can do that immediately.
David: Or solve a particular problem.

John: Right. This concept is a little tougher to grasp, but I do see them trying.

David: I also think there's something intrinsically valuable about giving back, about volunteering together, in conjunction with the story. That combination changes people's hearts, too. There's something really powerful about that.

Joe: As you guys think about the coming year, what's next in relation to your story?

David: I'm thinking about how we can leverage all this!

John: I think that the potential for the story to change over time does exist. However, when we were developing it, David and I worked hard to focus on the core things that wouldn't change over time rather than more transient items. That way, in the day-to-day battle of doing business, the story will help us overcome challenges because it's an ever-present reminder of our true core values. It helps you and the other people around you come to the same conclusions, because it is what we feel is right. I'll share another story with you real quick.

By now we're all very familiar with the reality that the economy took a nosedive in the late 2000s. On the unfortunate side, David and I gave people kind of a pass to underperform. I just kept telling people to do the right thing, but just telling them that didn't seem to click. It was more like sandpaper on glass. But once we had the story, doing the right thing became well-defined.

David: You just stirred something in my thoughts, John. In this sad economy, there are a lot of really good people available. I mean, there's a huge talent pool out there, but it's so big, which makes it difficult to find the right people. When you use the story to define the intrinsic characteristics and the values that you're looking for in your employees, you can vet people for those characteristics. I feel really, really good that we're on the right track with hiring good people now. That's huge.

John: There are also, quite frankly, a lot of not-so-good people available. So how do you differentiate them? How do you segregate them? How do you bring the good ones to light and leave the bad ones behind? That's where the story has value as well.

David: It may not ensure that you get a good new hire, but it certainly has to improve your probabilities.

John: Absolutely. And at the end of the day, we are going forward and living out our story. VibrAlign is a little company located in Richmond, Virginia. It's trying to have an impact on our small universe, and that small universe continues to grow. At a time when other businesses have not been hiring, we have. We've hired very good people over the last several years. We've added to our strength by those people, and going back to the title of your book, we're going to grow regardless.

David: I was talking about higher purpose earlier and this just popped into my head. We've started thinking bigger since undertaking this process. Now we're not only thinking about realigning our company, we're thinking we should realign America. I know that maybe it sounds a little corny, but I think we can have an impact on America. Honestly.

John: You know what, that is what America is about. If you listen to the news today, there's a lot of "anti-Americanism" out there, but most of that is politically focused. The reality is Americans want to work, Americans want to be creative, and Americans are competitive.

In the 1800s, we pushed out west. In the 1900s, we learned how to be an industrial force in the world, and we learned how to do it well. A lot of people have pointed us in the right direction, Henry Ford and Rockefeller among them. There's a long list of people who have done exactly what we're talking about here, and their over-arching attitude was this: You're not going to get in my way. No matter what you do, you're not going to get in my way. I'm going to grow.

Exercise: Planting the Seeds for Growth through Story

- Complete a "25 Reasons Why" exercise for your chosen career. Remember there are no wrong answers, but the answers must come from the heart. Then circle your top three reasons.
- Do another ""Twenty-Five Reasons Why" list, this time for your company, and circle the top three reasons.
- Create your own personal story, one that incorporates your big *why* from the above exercise. Write down your story and practice telling it to others: colleagues, employees, friends, and family members.
- Create the story for your company that incorporates the reasons from #2 above. The story should communicate why your organization exists, what you do, and how you do it, with emphasis on the *why*.
- Practice telling your company story and make adjustments as you note reactions.

Additional Resources

For more ways to plant the seeds for growth through Story, visit www.growregardless.com/book/story for a free training video.

Chapter 6

EMPLOYEE EXPERIENCE— MAKE THEM FEEL VALUED

A leader is best when people barely know he exists; when his work is done, his aim fulfilled, they will say: we did it ourselves.
—Lao Tzu

When I think about the ultimate employee experience, my mind jumps to my favorite restaurant, which takes such great care of its employees that its servers and chefs have stayed for a decade. I think of the family-run convenience store near my college campus, which was able to compete with the national chain across the street because its employees knew they were valued members of a team. But the best example I've ever seen wasn't by design. It was completely by happenstance when I signed up, along with ten other guys, to climb Tanzania's Mount Kilimanjaro in 2006. Where better to learn hands-on lessons about teamwork and leadership than in a five-day, real-world laboratory hanging off the side of a soaring mountain?

We were eleven men from all walks of life, ranging in age from twenty-eight to sixty. I was the youngest. One man, a member of the Sierra Club, knew everything there was to know about the great outdoors. Then there was me, who had never even camped before. The rest of our group fell somewhere between those two extremes.

We started our climb in a tropical jungle at 6,000 feet, headed for a snow-covered summit at more than 19,000 feet, where the temperatures range between zero and minus twenty degrees. We were accompanied by a group of porters, thirty-five Tanzanian men who would carry our equipment, feed us, help us set up, and break camp, and generally make our trip more enjoyable. In my research, I had read that climbers are asked to be careful how they treat the porters because if someone were to tip them really well or interact with them in an exceedingly friendly way, they might see that as the new norm and expect it from the next group. So there were clear standards in place designed to prevent anyone from upsetting the delicate balance of power between the climbers (the bosses) and the porters (the employees).

The porters were amazing people. They provided five-star service on one of the world's tallest mountains—no easy feat—and they did it with grace. They carried fifty-pound packs on their heads while we carried our little twenty-pound backpacks. They set up camp at each rest area before we arrived, which was amazing when you consider that they didn't break down the morning camp until we climbers were up and on our way. Then they would pack up, run past us (even though we had a head start of several hours!) and get to the next camp site well ahead of us, to have dinner ready and waiting. They went out of their way to ensure we were never without a full belly. They woke us every morning with tea outside our tents so we didn't have to wait until we got dressed. It was service with a smile, every time.

These men were incredibly warm and unassuming. When we spoke to them, they did their best to converse with their limited English. For days, we played this silly master/servant game, following the rules the excursion company had established. But as it turns out, all the climbers on this trip were community-minded, let's-go-save-the-world kind of people, and by the third day we decided we'd had enough of the status quo. We wanted to get to know these folks. Sure, we had been gracious with them throughout the climb in terms of thanking them for their hard work and asking if we could help with this or that. But that felt insufficient. What we came to understand was they didn't want our help. They wanted our respect. They wanted to feel valued.

Before dinner on that third evening, we took the head porter aside and told him we'd like to meet with all the porters. We wanted to introduce ourselves, but more importantly we wanted them to introduce themselves to us. We wanted to know their names, where each of them was from, what their job was and what they were passionate about. He nodded and went to gather the porters.

So there we were, 15,000 feet up the side of Mount Kilimanjaro, the eleven of us climbers sitting side-by-side facing a long line of porters sitting shoulder-to-shoulder. It was strangely tense. The first porter stood, his eyes averted.

"My name is David," he said quietly. "I am from Arusha. I carry the food."

We all greeted David and thanked him for his service. The next man got to his feet.

"I am Haki and I am from Tanga. I carry medicine. I have three sons," he said with shy pride.

We all laughed and applauded. The positive energy rose as the next man came forward, then the next and the next, until we came to the very last person—the smallest of all the porters. I will never forget him. He stood with his head held high, put his fist in the air, pounded his chest and said, "My name is Israel, and I carry the toilet!"

We leapt to our feet and started cheering and hugging Israel and the other porters, and the next thing we knew we were all doing this crazy dance around the campsite. We ended up hanging out with those guys for the next hour, celebrating our newfound—and heartfelt—connection. It was one of the coolest experiences I've ever had in my entire life.

This whole thing got even more interesting when one of our guys got severe altitude sickness the next day and couldn't make it any farther up the mountain. The porters went out of their way to make him comfortable and took him back to the base camp to wait for the rest of us to finish the climb.

They even gave him a special plaque at the closing luncheon, where the rest of us got certificates for making the summit.

We made a snap decision to treat the porters with compassion and empathy. I think they went the extra mile for us because we allowed ourselves to be vulnerable with them. We showed them that we cared and that we valued and respected them. We didn't plan it, but we took advantage of the chance to connect to those folks in a way that was really special, and we all reaped the benefits.

The Philosophy

If you give your employees an excellent experience, they will, in turn, give your clients an excellent experience. It's like the Golden Rule: Do unto others as you would have done unto you. This is probably the most intuitive part of **The eQ Growth Methodology**, but as my mentor once told me, "Sometimes, common sense principles aren't so common." We instinctively know that if we improve the way we treat our people, we'll get better results. The question is, why don't we?

I think it's because we have been taught since the dawn of time that the Golden Rule doesn't apply in the workplace; our employees are supposed to be subservient because they are inferior. The management philosophy rooted in the Industrial Revolution prescribed that employees need us more than we need them, and they'd better toe the line, or else.

Most of us know this is utter nonsense, yet we continue to cling to this dynamic. We've never rinsed ourselves of that outmoded residue from the old days, and it adversely affects both our corporate health and our national economy. With that in mind, consider this statement by Peter Drucker: "The purpose of business is to create and keep a customer." I love this quote, and given the point in history when Mr. Drucker thought it up, he was right. There was a time when the customer ruled with absolute authority, and the customer still rules today, *but so do your employees*. They have as many choices and, in some ways, are as powerful as your customers. They have more options from an employment perspective, and they have a louder voice than they have ever had. To grow, we must accept that this is true and begin to behave accordingly.

> *The purpose of business is to create and keep a customer.*
> —Peter Drucker

It's like physical fitness. We all know we'll live longer and enjoy life more if we exercise and eat right, yet many of us play a risky game of Russian roulette with our health by eating poorly, smoking, drinking to excess, and skipping workouts. Failing to treat your employees with dignity and respect is the same thing. We risk the well-being of our businesses by treating our employees badly, even though we know better.

Deny it at your peril. In a study entitled *Leadership That Gets Results*, author Daniel Goleman's research revealed that the fitness of the workplace climate (that is, employees' perception of the way management treats them) is responsible for nearly one-third of a company's financial results.[11] That's a big deal. Now factor in the cost of normal turnover, and it's clear that we have to do whatever we can to retain quality people. According to a Bureau of Labor Statistics study released in 2010, the average baby boomer has eleven jobs between the ages of eighteen and forty-four.[12] If someone stays with us for three to five years in this day and age, we would probably consider that a win. And despite the fact that the unemployment rate has hovered around 9 percent for several years, there are still plenty of job opportunities for competent go-getters. Losing a good person to one of your competitors hurts more than just your feelings. If you want to keep your best people so they can help your company grow regardless, you have to give them a remarkable experience. They're as important to your bottom line as your clients.

Why? Because your employees are responsible for carrying your story to your customers and for upholding the promises that story makes. They're the ones who look your customers in the eye and interact with them on a

---

11   Daniel Goleman, "Leadership That Gets Results," *Harvard Business Review* (March-April 2000): R00204.

12   US Bureau of Labor Statistics, News Release, 25 July 2012, accessed 8 Sept. 2012, http://www.bls.gov/news.release/pdf/nlsoy.pdf.

daily basis. If they are being treated shabbily, they're going to treat your customers shabbily. The Golden Rule we talked about earlier isn't just a nice old saying; it's a fact. Statistically, abused kids are more likely to abuse their own children someday. *We are affected and influenced by the manner in which we are led.* We can't escape that fact.

> Peter Drucker once noted that the distance between a leader and the average performer stays consistent. Therefore, it is easier to raise the performance of the leader and the average performance will follow.

Providing a great employee experience isn't about letting your employees run rampant or climbing trees at a one-time retreat. It isn't even about paying your employees a ton of money. *USA Today* conducts a poll every year that asks people why they stay in their jobs, and their relationship with their boss is usually one of the top two or three reasons, with salary further down the list. Sure, a fair wage is an important part of the picture, but paying someone well and treating them like dirt will not achieve the results necessary for growth. Recall the MIT study I discussed in Chapter 2 that explored the best ways to motivate people. Researchers now know that the old carrot-and-stick mentality is insufficient.

There are more meaningful ways to make people feel good about working with you and your company, and it all begins with a fresh mindset. Years ago, Southwest Airlines ran an ad that read "Employees First, Customers Second, Shareholders Third." It was a startling concept at the time. But it worked out so well for Southwest that other companies, large and small, have adopted that mindset and reaped the benefits. Those that haven't will continue to lose their best people. This is a big enough problem that Forbes.com put out a list of reasons why companies most often lose their best talent, including[13]:

---

13 Eric Jackson, "Top Ten Reasons Why Large Companies Fail to Keep Their Best Talent," *Forbes*, 24 Dec. 2011, accessed 28 Dec. 2011, www.forbes.com/sites/ericjackson/2011/12/14/top-ten-reasons-why-large-companies-fail-to-keep-their-best-talent/.

- Failing to capitalize on their employees' passions
- Inadequate annual review processes
- Lack of attention to career development
- Unstable company priorities or lack of vision
- Telling people how to do their jobs
- Not listening to input

The employee experience is about taking a stand for your people and making an effort to show them that they matter, and then giving them the tools and the freedom they need to get the job done. If you need a guidepost, here it is: *Treat your clients like employees and your employees like your clients.*

 If you need a guidepost, here it is: *Treat your clients like employees and your employees like your clients.*

This quote hit me as the way to go after my first Leadership 360, in which I solicited honest feedback from every one of my employees. I pride myself on being empathetic and compassionate, but I also pride myself on being a hard worker who's driven to succeed. At times, those qualities have been in conflict, most notably in 2006 when our training business was struggling and we created our consulting practice out of our need for more clients. I became our first consultant, personally handling ten clients and carrying more than $800,000 of billing in one year—something I don't recommend to anyone. I was 100 percent client-focused, 100 percent of the time. I even slept with my Blackberry on my chest so I would never miss a call.

But what I did miss was connecting to my team in a meaningful way. I thought they would see my hard work as a good example to follow, but instead they saw it as a slight. They felt like second fiddles to the clients. Occasionally, that's to be expected, but over time it caused my team to see me as uncaring. They told me I was out of touch, a bad listener and hard to work with . . . all the things I swore I'd never be as a leader. It was a real eye-opener for me.

Since then, I have worked very hard to be more attuned to my employees and to ensure they have an experience that is just as good as our customers' experience, so much so that the *Baltimore Business Journal* has honored us as one of the city's "Best Places to Work." When we won the award, the *Journal* asked me when we started doing great things like paying 100 percent of our employees' health insurance premiums, providing unlimited vacations, sponsoring volunteer days, and giving away the latest technology, including iPads, to our employees for personal use. My answer was that we've been doing this stuff since we started the company. The only thing new was my leadership approach. The moment I decided to make the employee experience my priority, the ground shifted under my feet.

Offering a remarkable employee experience is liberating in one sense, but it comes with great responsibility. There are many examples of winning companies that have taken that responsibility to heart and profited greatly as a result. With its people-centered policy of "employees first, clients second, shareholders third," Southwest Airlines managed to grow revenue by 31 percent in the lackluster economy of 2010.[14] The first US airline to offer profit-sharing to employees in the 1970s, Southwest has earned the following distinctions, among many others[15]:

- The lowest ratio of complaints per passengers boarded of all major U.S. carriers since record-keeping began in 1987
- The top-rated airline for customer service in 2011, according to *Consumer Reports*
- The top-rated airline in five categories by Zagat in 2010
- Paying 138 consecutive quarterly dividends to its shareholders

---

14   Mark Harden, "Southwest Airlines Slows Growth as Costs Rise," *Denver Business Journal*, 4 Aug. 2011, accessed 14 Oct. 2011, www.bizjournals.com/denver/news/2011/08/04/southwest-airlines-slows-growth-as.html.

15   Southwest Airlines, "Fact Sheet," accessed 13 Oct. 2011, www.southwest.com/html/about-southwest/history/fact-sheet.html.

By putting employees first, it's clear that everyone wins at Southwest.

The airline proves that when you treat employees with respect and show them, in meaningful ways, that you value their humanity, your business will grow. What can you do to lead in a way that's more likely to achieve that growth? How do you live this "remarkable employee experience" idea fully and without question? How do you ensure that if your employees were put in a room one by one and asked if they feel valued, they would overwhelmingly answer *yes*?

You give them these seven things:

1. *Clarity*
2. *Certainty*
3. *Compassion*
4. *Consistency*
5. *Commitment*
6. *Collaboration*
7. *Community*

The Process

Clarity is the first thing your people want and deserve. They want and deserve to know *where* the company is going, exactly *what* they're being asked to do, *why* they are doing it, and *how* their efforts contribute to the company's success. They don't want just a piece of paper with a job description on it. They want a dialogue. They want an exchange of information and ideas in which they can offer input and believe their voices are being heard. They deserve that level of clarity *at all times*. Not just once a year at a company event or once a quarter with a newsletter. They want an ongoing, honest, clear, two-way conversation about where you're going as a company and the specific things they can do to help you get there.

The second thing you can give employees is a sense of **certainty**. In these turbulent times, people crave reassurance. It's human nature. Think about it: All of us have probably watched at least one movie more than once this year. Even though you knew how the movie was going to end, you watched it again because you like the sureness of it. There is no fear or doubt about the outcome.

So if people are comforted by knowing the outcome of a two-hour movie, imagine how much they'd appreciate having some level of certainty around their career. Remember, doubt is only good when it's a question of *how* you're going to get where you're going. From a leadership perspective, if you're giving people doubt about *where* you're all going, *what* is most important, or *why* you're doing this work, you're allowing a level of uncertainty that your people might not be able to power through. Sure, there are still companies closing and banks failing and you can't predict the future. But your team will be able to stand the uncertainty of the things you can't control if you've given them a firm grip on the stuff you can control, like your collective values and your organizational mission.

The third C is **compassion**. Jim Collins discussed this in *Good to Great*, in which he wrote that compassion is one of the most striking differences between the most successful CEOs and the rest of the pack. Compassion is showing people that you care, you're there for them, you think of them as human beings and not just worker bees. As Stephen Covey wrote, compassion is about listening with your mind, body and heart.

Remember the Native American tradition of the talking stick? Every night, the tribe gathered around the campfire to tell their stories of the day. The person whose turn it was to talk would hold a stick while he spoke, and he would only pass that stick on to the next person when he felt sure that the tribe understood, empathized, and valued what he had just said. It's a tradition that many Native Americans still carry on today. All those studies of what motivates people are just modern-day confirmation of something they have known since the dawn of time: All that each of us really wants is to be heard and to feel valued.

The next C is **consistency**, which has three prongs: consistency of message, consistency of communications method, and consistency in action. When an employee comes to you with a problem or a question, do they receive consistent statements from you? Are they going to get the same sort of answer tomorrow that you gave them today? One approach to this is not getting too emotional; you don't ride the highs too high or the lows too low. It's about responding to a situation versus reacting.

For the method of communications, there must be a clear and consistent channel of interaction between executive leadership, managers, and employees. This could be a daily phone call, a weekly meeting, a monthly check-in, a quarterly review or an annual town hall meeting.

Last, are your actions reliable? Do you walk the talk? In the words of the poet Kahlil Gibran, are you a stable bow capable of sending your arrows "swift and far"? Your team craves a steady hand and drama-free leadership.

Commitment is the next C. Your people need to feel that not only are you certain, caring, consistent, and clear, but also that you are the most committed person in the room. You're the one who sets the commitment bar. Monkey see, monkey do. If your employees see that you're willing to walk through a wall to get to where you want to go as a company—to live out your story—they'll be likely to at least pick up a hammer and try to knock a hole in that wall, too. But if you're only willing to tap on the wall, if you're not displaying sufficient firmness or resolve, your people will sense that and start to act wishy-washy, too. What people want to see is an amazing amount of commitment from their leadership; they want to know that no matter what happens, you'll find a way. That no matter what, you'll never give up. That we may not always be sure of how we're going to get there, but we're committed to going and that's that. People trust and are inspired by committed leaders. But lukewarm leaders? Not so much.

The sixth C is **collaboration**. Collaborative leaders don't care who gets the credit or who comes up with the right answer. Instead, they foster an environment in which the questions are what matter and rank and title are irrelevant when it comes to finding solutions. It's about challenging the status quo and getting people thinking about how the team can win, not how "I" can win. Collaborative leaders eradicate the old us-versus-them mentality because they know that people need to feel connected.

Folks who telecommute or sit in a lonely cubicle eight hours a day will tell you in a heartbeat that a sense of connection is powerful, whether it's through a video conference at the end of the week or a meeting in which the team gets together to brainstorm and build on each other's energy. It's just like a football game: After each play, the teammates huddle and collaborate. *What are we going to do on this next play? How we can best move this ball forward toward our goal?* Your employees need those collaborative huddles, too.

You probably won't find the last C, **community**, in many leadership books, but it's something entrepreneurs are starting to become passionate about. Pink references it in his book *Drive*, calling it Motivation 3.0. Napoleon Hill in *Think and Grow Rich* talked about how people function at a more intense level of passion when they understand that the work is about more than themselves.

The concept is about operating from a place of higher purpose, for the greater good. Is your company involved in making a difference (and not just from a philanthropic perspective)? Are you making the world a better place? Are you recycling? Do you sponsor a food drive around Thanksgiving? Do you ever get out of the office to give back as a team, like participating in a Walk for the Cure, a Habitat for Humanity project, or a child-mentoring program?

I can tell you from experience that the companies that participated in b4students, including my own, experienced amazingly positive outcomes as a result. Going through the four-year process of helping kids successfully go from the ninth grade to graduation increased retention, morale, productivity, passion, and loyalty in all the participating companies. Generally speaking, when those things are up, profits will follow.

A good friend of mine once said that Mother Teresa was a selfish person. The statement shocked me, because clearly Mother Teresa was one of the most self-sacrificing people who ever lived. But he went on to explain that when you give your time and talents to the community as Mother Teresa did, what you get back is exponentially greater than anything you give. Generosity is not a selfless act, because you get such immense rewards in return. I'm not talking about a *quid pro quo* where I get money or good press for doing something nice. I'm talking about the way it makes you feel inside. If you give your team ample opportunities to experience those good feelings together, you'll become stronger as a unit. You'll create positive energy around your team—energy that will naturally pass on to your customers.

There are three ways to make the Seven Cs part of your company culture and have a positive impact regardless of your size, your industry or the economy. The first is by revamping your annual review process. Now, some of you might be saying, "We don't have an annual review process," and that's problem number one. Some of you might say, "We have an annual review process, but it's not consistent," and that's problem number two. Others among you might say, "Yeah, we have an annual review, but our employees hate it and our managers think it's a chore." That's problem number three, and that's where we're going to start.

There are several things wrong with the typical annual review process. The first is that it's called an "annual" review, and it shouldn't be. Getting together with your employees two to four times a year to talk about their strategic direction, their career path, and where they're headed as employees inside your organization is most effective from a best practices standpoint, because it makes it easier to follow up and hold people accountable. Another mistake is looking at employee reviews as something you *have* to do rather than something you *get* to do. As author Wayne Dyer says, "When you change the way you look at things, the things you look at change," so if you can think about reviewing as a way to help your company and its people become more successful, then perhaps you'll begin to see it as a privilege and not a chore.

The second way to make the Seven Cs part of your culture is to ask for feedback from your employees. We used to conduct what we called "employee satisfaction surveys," but the new buzzword is "voice of the employee surveys." Today, you can go on SurveyMonkey.com, plunk down less than $30 and create your own employee survey to send to your people. To make it really easy, you can create the survey using the Gallup Q12[16], a series of twelve standard questions that's been around since the 1990s for assessing employee satisfaction. You can ask employees to rate their

16   Feedback for Real, *Gallup Business Journal*, 23 Nov. 2011, http://gmj.gallup.com/content/811/feedback-real.aspx.

agreement or disagreement with those statements on a scale of one to five. It will take you less than half an hour to set up the survey and send it to your employees. That's an investment of less than thirty minutes to ask your team what's most important to them.

Now, two things to consider before you go running off to do a survey. You should not conduct a survey internally, which means you should hire an outside consultant to manage it for you. This sounds like a selfish plug for a company like ours, but I don't make that plug lightly. You want your employees to know for sure that the survey is anonymous, it is tamper-proof, and they can give honest answers. Otherwise, you'll get less than candid responses, and when that happens, everyone loses.

Second, there's only one thing worse than not asking your people for feedback, and that's asking for feedback and then not doing anything about it. There must be a firm commitment to work through whatever the employees kick back to you. You must be willing to bring the responses into the light of day and deal with them as a team, even when it's not pretty—*especially* when it's not pretty. That's what collaboration is all about.

The last thing to consider relative to the employee experience is the idea of coaching. We're all about accountability and managing, but many companies don't properly coach their people. Why? Because they don't know how. The word "coach" is so simple, and it seems so simple to do. Many of us have played sports and watched what our coaches did. Some of us may even be Little League coaches ourselves. But think of it this way: If I were to hold a scalpel in my hand, it would be no more use to me than a pen knife because I have no idea how to do surgery. When a doctor holds a scalpel, however, it's serious business. When I hold a pen, I'm just doodling and playing around. When an attorney holds a pen to write an air-tight contract, he makes art.

The same is true of coaching at this level. When you give someone the responsibility of being a coach without the proper training or direction, they're likely to just play around. They're likely to do what they've seen done in a movie or on a TV show—or worse, to do what was done to them.

Employee Experience in Practice: Chris Krause and the National Collegiate Scouting Association

Motivation to build the NCSA came from Chris Krause's own experiences as a high-school athlete in the college recruiting process. Today, NCSA connects student-athletes with coaches and scholarships to help them make the most of both sports and education. Krause has built an incredibly strong team culture based on accountability, communication, empowerment of employees and, along the way, a few tough decisions.

Joe: Why don't you give me the formal introduction and history of NCSA?

Chris: NCSA started with the dream of a fourth-grader who wanted to play college sports, and that was me. I had a role model who was playing high-school ball, and the seed was planted in my brain at an early age that I might be able to play sports in college in return for an education. In fifth or sixth grade, I started writing down goals with the hope that one day I could play sports. Eventually, I was able to make that dream a reality and got a full ride to Vanderbilt for football.

It wasn't until about 1982, when I entered the recruiting process, that I started getting letters from colleges. I knew that was the first sign that I was pretty good and colleges would be interested in me. I made Tom Lemming's book in being recognized as one of the top players in the country. By making that list, I got tons of letters and everyone was telling me I was going to be the next Mike Singletary of the era. When I got all the letters, I just assumed the scholarships would be lined up. When my senior year came around and other kids were getting visits and offers, I still had that big box of letters and I didn't know what to do with it. My coaches didn't have a lot of input. I realized there was a big gap in the process, especially when I started calling coaches and they said, "We didn't know you were interested in us, so we need a video." My dad and I had to rent video equipment to make highlight tapes. I started sending them to colleges and started getting airplane tickets back in the mail and making official visits to colleges. It was a last-minute thing. A lot of coaches already had commitments and a lot of schools had already filled up their scholarship offers. This was early in my senior year, so I got lucky that I ended up getting a scholarship. But had I not gotten involved myself and had my parents not gotten involved, that would have passed me by. So that's how that whole concept started.

I went to Vanderbilt, majored in human development and started helping kids locally with the scholarship process. Then I went home to Chicago and started doing it the old-fashioned way. We'd write a résumé up and I'd send it out to colleges. It worked to some degree, but it was cumbersome and took a long time. When technology started coming around, I realized it could be done more efficiently and for a lot less money than it would cost parents to do it themselves. Once we started building relationships with colleges and getting information on kids on a national level, we started coupling that with the power of education. That became our lead generator. We were able to get a lot of people to understand what was at stake and get them to start early. We were only working with the kids who were good enough and making sure they were realistic. That's how NCSA started.

It was a merger of education, technology, and empowering these leaders through sports, by teaching them what they needed to do at an early age so they could set goals and get the grades they needed and we could connect them with the college coaches and help them know what to do after the connections were made. Those were all things that most kids don't know about and a lot of their parents don't know.

Joe: When you think about way you built your company from a cultural perspective, what were some of the things you translated from your personal story and from the company's mission to your company's culture?

Chris: As a sophomore in college, I took a course on corporate culture, so I was aware of corporate culture at an early age. I was fortunate to understand how important culture was in an organization. I realized, as I started to read a lot of books on the enduring, built-to-last companies, that companies have their heroes, their mavens, their stories, and they're bigger than just the bottom line. People want to be part of a team. They want to know where we're going and how we're going to get there. They want to know their seat on the bus or their position on the team, and they want to know they're in a safe place, that it's okay to fail. Failure is encouraged as long as you learn from it. Being in a safe place, versus a place where there's fear and failure, is something that's frowned upon, I think that's a big part of culture. And the last thing is they want to have fun. People like to be together, so having fun in a team environment. These are the principles we use at NCSA.

Joe: What are some of the biggest challenges you have had from an employee engagement perspective?

Chris: It all revolves around getting the right people on the bus in the first place. That's where core values come in. Our core values have evolved over the years. We've gone from two employees to over 300 now. We've gotten a lot of input from our athleadership team. That's a word I invented—athleadership. The definition is empowering leaders through the life lessons of sports. Our core values are spelled in the acronym TEAM LG: team, education, all-in attitude and all-out work ethic, making your mark, leading by example, and giving back. That's what we look for and we actually measure our team on all six of those.

Getting the right people in was the initial challenge. The other challenge is when you're growing as fast as we are—we've had close to triple-digit growth a lot of years—being flexible enough to have people shift as they max out talent levels. Being able to keep a career path growing at that rate is tough, because a lot of people are at the forefront of that career path and they're bumping their heads in areas that might be outside their skill set. When you put all those high-producing, high-drive people together, you get a lot of growth, but with a lot of growth come a lot of challenges, which forces you to change the lineup along the way. When things don't work, we have to quickly recover and make the decision to move forward, to move the person out of the position and give them another task so we don't continue down the wrong path.

Joe: Any other challenges you can think of?

Chris: Half of our company is not in Chicago, so keeping our culture together has been a big challenge. We've done a lot of work on Skype and using technology to bring the team together. We do a monthly huddle where we get everyone together for a half-hour and do a company update. We do a company newsletter, a lot of digital videos and webinars, and a national meeting. We have a monthly scout meeting and our Tuesday 10 o'clock meetings still go on today, twelve years later, at the exact time and place as when we first set them up.

Joe: Was there a defining moment for you that reconfirmed that culture was the most important?

Chris: As the core values became more defined, the people who weren't in alignment with them started to stand out more. The more they stood out, the easier it was to identify actions that weren't in alignment. They were in high leadership positions, but eventually, because I was listening to the employees, these people ended up being let go. It was hard to let a few of those people go because they had been with the company for so long, but when their actions weren't congruent with the culture, the choice was easy. We couldn't let people stay on that the rest of the team did not respect in terms of alignment with culture. Some of the toughest decisions became the easiest decisions and ultimately turned out to be the best decisions because the company flourished.

Joe: The people that helped start the company aren't necessarily the people that are going to help you grow the company. Those become very tough decisions for entrepreneurs. You build the business around you and it becomes a family, in a sense.

Chris: A lot of people have partners, relatives, best friends in the business, and as the company grows and the culture is defined, not everyone is as aligned as you were in the beginning. Eventually, in order to grow, there has to be alignment and tough decisions have to be made. What was best for the company isn't always best for a few individuals that may have been along since the beginning. Letting them go let everyone know how committed we are to culture and to doing things the right way. I've heard from other companies, too, those are benchmark decisions. I haven't heard one time where someone said, "Gosh, I fired someone and I wish I hadn't." It's always, "I wish I would have done it earlier." If you think they're not in alignment, chances are your instincts are right.

Joe: When you think about some of your peers, what makes you "get it" when you see a lot of your peers not understanding the impact of a healthy culture on a company?

Chris: One of the things I do is measure culture on a scale of one to ten. One of our top five priorities is to keep our culture at a nine-plus. Granted, we're not always at a nine-plus, but I check with my executive team and our leadership team and we are constantly surveying our employees to see how we're doing and how we as a leadership team are living up to our core values. Are we putting the team first and taking care of our people? Are we making sure we're putting them in an environment where they can thrive? Are we continually educating ourselves and getting better and bringing world-class, cutting-edge ideas and philosophies?

We have a dream board where everyone puts their dreams up and we make a point to measure every month whether people achieving their goals. People who want to buy a house, are they buying houses? People who want Christian Louboutin shoes, are they saving up to do that? Are they losing fifteen pounds in a year and working out? There's a lot more than the bottom dollar that our team wants, so to measure and put things on the board that are bigger than what money gives you at the end of the paycheck is something we memorialize and celebrate. One guy wanted to take his wife to Paris. I just got a picture of him underneath the Arc de Triomphe with his wife.

As an organization, we're looking at the team as a whole and as individuals to see whether they are achieving their individual goals and how we can help them. By measuring that, I feel we've been able to let the employees know we care. Every month, when someone stands up in front of the team and talks about how they got to do something they never thought they'd do, it gets them out of their comfort zone. One girl wanted to see Chipper Jones' last ballgame in Atlanta and we sent her out there. She's sitting out there on the field smiling ear to ear. That helps us continue to build our culture and it builds loyalty.

Joe: How does having a clear vision help this process?

Chris: Almost everybody joined NCSA because of the vision. We don't pay the most salary, but we do, I think, have as clear a vision, if not the clearest vision, that people want to be part of. That vision is building the world's first athleadership network and connecting all these athletes, and not just for the short term of trying to get them into college. With 50,000 student-athletes in college now, employers are starting to realize the benefits of hiring former athletes. We constantly have people tour our campus and our scouting center, and they see what is happening and say, "How do I get a culture like that?" I tell them to recruit athletes with high drive and a high work ethic, great-attitude kids who want to be part of something big, and then train the heck out of them and teach them what their role is and where they're going. It's the vision that gets them in. By measuring our results on a daily, weekly, quarterly, and yearly basis, we're holding ourselves accountable from the top down. Ten years ago, you helped me write my 2012 vision to be a $50 million company, and we're going to do that this year.

Joe: What is the first thing you tell folks when they don't get the financial impact of culture and they don't get that people are their most important asset?

Chris: What gets people fired up is passion. Passion is what drives our mission and our vision and our values. If they're getting up to get a paycheck every day, this isn't the right place for them. We put our kids first and our families and the ultimate success of our people. These families are putting their kids' lives in our hands; it's a big commitment. People have got to bring their A game every day because if we don't bring our A game in our industry, kids lose opportunities and don't get educated. That's a lot of positive pressure we put on our people to perform because people are putting their kids, their most precious asset, in our hands to make sure they are able to maximize this athletic recruiting process. So the idea of having a vision that is bigger and has some emotion attached to it, we found, has been our formula for success, because people will do a lot more.

If you look at all the great performances in team sports, people work harder for a teammate a lot of times than they will for themselves. That's the same thing we've done at NCSA by having those accountabilities and expectations. By having people who do not want to let their teammates down, that culture has gotten us a lot more value per employee and a lot more effort because there's a purpose for being there. It's important to make sure our employees know what a difference they're making, whether they're editing a video or putting something in Quickbooks—they can see how all these moving parts are driving toward athleadership and empowering leaders through sports. I just spoke with a CEO who played football at the University of San Diego, and he sees that student-athletes aren't afraid to fail and they can handle adversity. They're high-drive and they learn how to keep their egos in check and be part of a team. A big part of our success has been recruiting on those values.

Joe: Over the last ten years, you have built a $50 million company. What are some of the challenges you see on the horizon as you think about plateaus for the business around culture?

Chris: As you get more people and more moving parts, keeping a bigger team together on the same page. Communication is going to be everything. Making sure people are connecting with the culture, seeing that leadership is adhering to the core values and seeing the company giving back in the community. We have athleadership grants, and part of our mission is to make sure every qualified student-athlete has access to this network. We have a bounty of ten percent of the kids who are going to get in either for free, through partnerships, sponsorships or our foundation, or at a reduced rate, because they are financially challenged. We're putting our money where our mouth is and the company sees it. We've never turned down a qualified family for financial reasons.

Everyone knows that's a big part of me personally, because I came from a part of the country that was really blue-collar. Our culture stems from my experience that on my high-school team, everybody was good enough to play somewhere and I was the only kid that got a scholarship. Some of those kids are no longer with us. Some are in jail. I know what a difference it would make in my community of North Chicago if we had twenty people, instead of just one, who went on to get an education, have scholarships, and come back into that community as role models. I know more kids would be alive today and there would be a lot more good fathers and good role models in that community. That's probably the most critical element that's driven us, is that passion for making sure we're giving back and helping those kids.

Joe: At the end of the day, what do you want to be known for?

Chris: One of the signs of leadership, in my view, is how many other leaders have you helped grow. If we can teach companies and teach leaders how the lessons of sports translate into life lessons that are going to make them better humans and help others grow, that's what I want to be known for and what I want NCSA to be known for. With 50,000 kids coming out of colleges, our mantra is commit, succeed and lead. That mantra means commit to doing the right thing. Succeed with a meaningful college degree so that you can take the tools with you, from your education and your sports experience, into your community and your next team, wherever that career takes you. Be leaders in those organizations and in your community.

The athleadership movement is teaching families these life lessons that they take with them for the rest of their lives: how to translate those lessons of failure recovery, of going from a third-string linebacker to a second-string linebacker to a starting linebacker, of going from a 2.0 GPA and working your tail off for a 3.0 GRA and graduating with a meaningful degree, of learning from the loss as well as the win, of learning how to treat people and how to win with dignity and lose with dignity—all those things are part of athleadership.

Joe: What are the biggest lessons you've learned from your employees?

Chris: The biggest lesson we've learned from our employees is that they need to be listened to. We need to acknowledge there are a lot of smart people, give them opportunities, empower them to use their talents and make them feel they can make a play in a safe environment. That has led us to having a lot of smart people grow in the company, from the bottom up versus the top down. The more we delegate down, the more we free people up. There's so much talent that allows our most talented people to take on new responsibilities and roles to help grow the company.

One of our corporate logos is the baton, which symbolizes the hand-off. When you hand something off, you trust that hand-off. In track and field, if someone drops the baton, you are disqualified. The whole team loses. To trust the hand-off, you're going to hand off to someone who is going to do as well as, if not better than, you. You feel comfortable that you're handing off a task you've mastered and that frees you up to do more. In our culture, employees are getting that leadership means developing more leaders, and the only way you can develop more leaders is to hand off more responsibility. Obviously, you then measure and monitor and coach them up. Having that environment has been huge—listening, delegating, giving more responsibility sooner, and letting people know it's okay to fail. One of the big things we embrace at NCSA is the ability to trust and hand off the baton so we can continue to grow as a team.

Exercise: Planting the Seeds for Growth through Employee Experience

To be a good leader, you must provide your management team and your frontline staff with the 7 Cs. The first step is to do a self-assessment of how well you exhibit these qualities, where you excel and where you need improvement.

To do so, answer the questions below using the following grading scale:

5: Strongly Agree
4: Agree
3: Somewhat Agree
2: Somewhat Disagree
1: Disagree
0: Strongly Disagree

FOR YOU:

1. My vision for where we are going is clear.
2. I have an overwhelming sense of certainty about where we are going.
3. I truly feel compassionate for my employees, what they bring to the table, and where they are on their journeys.
4. I keep my word to my management team.
5. I feel as though I will find a way to succeed regardless of the circumstances.
6. I often ask others for their input in making decisions.
7. I operate from a higher purpose.

FOR YOUR MANAGEMENT TEAM:

1. My management team acts in accordance with my vision.
2. My management team never wavers in the face of difficult times.
3. My management team demonstrates compassion for their employees during the good and bad times.
4. My management team keeps their one-on-one and team meetings with direct reports without fail.
5. My management team demonstrates commitment to the company, their growth and the growth of their direct reports.
6. My management team works well together.

7. My management team is actively involved in the community and contributes new ideas for involvement.

FOR YOUR FRONTLINE STAFF:
1. The employees on my team talk about the vision regularly.
2. There is an overwhelming sense of stability among the employees.
3. Our environment is one that is open and transparent in which employees feel as though they can communicate how they are feeling, where they are, and what they need help with.
4. The employees feel a strong sense of structure regarding message, processes, and meeting rhythm.
5. Our turnover is above average (meaning little turnover) for our industry.
6. Our departments are "silo-free."
7. As a company, we value community and actively participate in "give back days" at least once per year.

Add up your numeric answers and find your result on this scale:

85 to 105:	Exceptional
64 to 84:	Above average
43 to 63:	Average (take notice of areas for improvement)
22 to 42:	Needs improvement (take notice of areas for improvement and commit to improving)
0 to 21:	Not acceptable and complete revamp is critical

Performance Reviews

You must assess your current performance review process to understand what improvements need to be made. Answer the following statements with **Yes**, **Sometimes**, or **No**:

1. I consistently do performance reviews with my management team.
2. The management team consistently does performance reviews with our frontline staff.

3. The feedback about the performance reviews has been positive.

4. Each employee and manager knows what they are being held accountable for.

5. The frequency of the performance reviews is more than once per year.

6. The scoring system is a numeric scale with clearly defined definitions for each number.

7. The management team has been given training/coaching on how to conduct a positive performance review.

8. The employees look forward to their performance reviews because they get good feedback that is critical to their success.

9. There is a reward tied to exceptional or good performance.

10. The structure and processes are clearly defined.

If you answered **Yes** most of the time, consider keeping your existing performance review process.

If you answered **Sometimes** most of the time or often, consider digging in to the areas that aren't a firm **Yes**.

If you answered **No** to any question, you should immediately make changes.

Additional Resources

For more ways to plant the seeds for growth through Employee Experience, visit www.growregardless.com/book/empexp for a free training video.

Chapter 7

A Remarkable Client Experience—The Unconditional Guarantee

There are no traffic jams along the extra mile.
—Roger Staubach

While conducting a training recently, I asked three hundred people how many of them had had a remarkable customer experience in the last thirty days. Not an experience in which a company met or even exceeded their expectations, but an exchange in which a company gave them a truly remarkable experience. Only 20 percent of the people in that room could actually remember a recent remarkable experience.

And here's the gem. When I asked them who gave them that remarkable experience, it was never big shots like Starbucks, Southwest, or Nordstrom. It was the local dry cleaner who dropped everything to help them sew on a button. It was the hardware store clerk who helped a gentleman put together a leaf blower and then walked him out to the car and helped him load it into the trunk. It was the experience of a couple who made a dinner reservation and mentioned that it was their anniversary, and when they showed up, the chef was the one who served every course of their meal.

What made these experiences remarkable wasn't giving something away or offering a major discount. It wasn't based on a Super Bowl ad or some crazy national marketing campaign. These companies didn't hire consultants and pay them millions of dollars to figure this out. It was just people going the extra mile. It was people showing that they cared. It was folks being empathetic with their clients. It was about listening. It was about all the things we know we should be doing, but we're just not doing often enough.

It was the seventh game of the 1998 Johns Hopkins football season, and we were playing Dickinson College at our home stadium. We were up by a couple of points, with minutes left to play, and Dickinson had the ball. It was fourth down with two yards to go. My defensive teammates and I had to hold the line, but there was more at stake than a single game. We were shaping up to be the winningest team in our university's history. In more than a century, no Hopkins team had ever won more than seven games in a season and certainly never four years in a row (I'm proud to say that more recently, my alma mater has been ranked tenth nationwide in Division III play). The only thing between us and the record books was a scrappy Dickinson offense.

My teammates and I lined up, focused and ready. The center hiked the ball and the quarterback tossed a quick pass to the running back. He caught it, put his head down and barreled toward me. I had to stop him. Even though I knew it was dangerous, I put my head down and ran toward him as hard as I could. We hit each other full force, head-to-head . . . and the next thing I remember, I was being strapped to a board with dozens of people around me, my stepmother screaming and crying, and my dad looking more scared than I had ever seen him. I couldn't feel my hands or feet. I was paralyzed.

Sirens blaring, an ambulance rushed me to Baltimore's Shock Trauma Hospital. This place is world-renowned. Shock

Trauma saves many people who would have died in a regular hospital, because they have a system that works. When I arrived, they wheeled me into a large room with curtains between each patient. Next to me was a guy who had been shot three times and a ninety-year-old woman who had fallen down the stairs. Buzzers went off, beepers were paged and suddenly ten people in scrubs descended upon me, cutting off my uniform and asking questions. But instead of poking and prodding me, the doctors, several of them, came in and said, "Okay, here's what we're going to do." They took the time to educate me and help me think through what was happening. Their bedside manner was beyond excellent. They talked to me about football, and they brought in my parents even though it was probably against the rules. Their exceptional care calmed me and took me to a totally different place mentally, emotionally, and physically. And this was not a slow day for them, remember, there was a guy dying in the next bed.

It was a remarkable contrast to what I had seen in other hospitals, although I could rationalize those experiences by remembering the pressure the doctors and nurses were under to get to the next patient, to deal with the next emergency, to put out the next fire. People's lives were on the line, after all. But still, at Shock Trauma they took time to sit down with me and my parents and really relate to us. That's why today, when someone tries to tell me they are too busy to give their customers a remarkable experience, I have to respectfully disagree. If a hospital handling life-threatening emergencies can find the time, I think everyone can. Luckily, mine was a case of the bark being much worse than the bite. I was diagnosed with a concussion, a sprained neck, and what they call a "stinger." I was not paralyzed; I just had pinched my spinal cord, which sent a numb feeling to the rest of my body. It wasn't long before the feeling came back to my extremities. There are no words to describe my relief when I realized my paralysis was only temporary.

Once the medical team was certain I was going to be okay, they put me in a huge neck brace and began my discharge process. They recommended places for physical therapy and explained how to make sure there was no instability in my neck for the next thirty days. We discussed how often I would return for follow-up visits, and they suggested I get second opinions if I had any doubts about my diagnosis or treatment. The staff spent an incredible amount of time educating us, going above and beyond the typical hospital discharge experience. I remember thanking them, and their response was, "No, thank you. You've been such a great patient. We are so relieved this was only a big scare."

Yes, they thanked me for giving them the opportunity to treat me. It was a remarkable experience to be given such care, empathy, and respect. Without a doubt, Shock Trauma lived up to its reputation as Baltimore's place for superior emergency medical care.

The Philosophy

Like football seasons and fiscal years, our business teams have their ups and downs, too. If you expect to post a win and not a loss, it is imperative that you maintain your fan base and preserve the integrity of your network. One way for a business to preserve its steady following, and perhaps even grow it, is by keeping its word. At my company, "Keep your word" is our number one value, and our team has agreed on three behaviors in regard to living it out and giving our clients the ultimate experience every time:

1. Make your commitments realistically.
2. Follow through on your promises completely.
3. Display integrity and accountability to the extreme.

The ultimate client experience begins as a philosophy that aligns all employees in the relentless pursuit of ensuring every client gets what was promised in the organizational story. The result: Clients can and do express exactly why they patronize the organization. It is essential that everyone in the company—from top executive leadership throughout the organization to the frontline staff—understands it, owns it, and drives it. To have the desired effect, the philosophy must be consistent from division to division, regardless of the solutions offered or the type of clients served.

Why? Because after every customer interaction we have, the client will ask himself or herself this question: *Did that experience meet my expectations?* If the answer is no, we're in trouble. If the answer is yes, we may still be in trouble because simply *meeting* expectations is insufficient in our new-new reality.

Customer Experience Affects the Bottom Line

Buying More Products	**$65** Million
Reduction in Churn	**$116** Million
Word of Mouth	**$103** Million
	$248 Million

Customer experience annual revenue change from a modest shift in customer experience for a $10 billion company.

The way I see it, there are three levels of favorable customer service. You can meet the customer's needs, you can exceed them, or you can make their experience remarkable. In today's marketplace, if you merely meet a customer's needs, you're not doing anything noteworthy. Simply meeting a customer's expectations doesn't guarantee a long-term relationship or referral business. It doesn't guarantee anything. Meeting needs is vanilla.

> The way I see it, there are three levels of favorable customer service. You can meet the customer's needs, you can exceed them or you can make their experience remarkable. In today's marketplace, if you merely meet a customer's needs, you're not doing anything noteworthy.

Let's say you exceed my expectations. That's better than meeting them, but still, am I going to rave about you on Facebook later today? How many status updates can we have about the excellent tuna sandwich at your restaurant? It's just not meaningful anymore. It's not going to turn anyone into an ambassador for your establishment.

For the most part, our society is well past the first rung on the poverty ladder. Most of us already have sufficient food, clothing, shelter, and clean water; now we're looking for *experiences*. Your customers are seeking remarkable, outstanding, one-of-a-kind moments. Good is never going to be good enough again.

If we want to grow regardless, we have to move to an economy of unconditional guarantee. That's right, unconditional. Now that's remarkable. No more long infomercials with all the slick-talking qualifiers. No more disclaimers in fine print on the bottom of the screen. No qualifiers. We've said this from the beginning at entreQuest: If you're not happy with our services, we'll write you a check back. And we mean it. That's what it takes to succeed in today's marketplace.

We're not the only company going that extra mile. I'm a loyal customer of Zappos online shoe store because they offer free shipping—every day. No matter how much or how little you're buying. You can send the merchandise back as much as a year after purchasing it, and Zappos even picks up the tab for return shipping. Unconditional returns are also a big reason why I shop at Nordstrom. I've bought several shirts there and ended up not liking them, so I took them back without tags or receipts—even after wearing them once!—and Nordstrom gave me my money back, no questions asked.

And check out this fun email I received after making an online purchase from CD Baby:

> Your CDs have been gently taken from our CD Baby shelves with sterilized contamination-free gloves and placed onto a satin pillow.
>
> A team of 50 employees inspected your CDs and polished them to make sure they were in the best possible condition before mailing.
>
> Our packing specialist from Japan lit a candle and a hush fell over the crowd as he put your CDs into the finest gold-lined box that money can buy.
>
> We all had a wonderful celebration afterwards and the whole party marched down the street to the post office where the entire town of Portland waved "Bon Voyage!" to your package, on its way to you, in our private CD Baby jet on this day, Sunday, December 11th.
>
> I hope you had a wonderful time shopping at CD Baby. We sure did.
>
> Your picture is on our wall as "Customer of the Year." We're all exhausted but can't wait for you to come back to CDBABY. COM!
>
> Thank you once again,
>
> Derek Sivers, President, CD Baby

Those kinds of unconditional guarantees and personalized communications may seem excessive, unreasonable, and unnecessary. It's hard to believe any company could survive operating that way, turning over the reins to their customers like that and spending so much time and effort to connect. Yet here I am, a screaming fan, telling the world how much I love Zappos, Nordstrom, and CD Baby. It's likely that a few of you will now patronize those businesses just because I told you about my remarkable experiences with them.

This concept is not exactly new. In the 1990s, James Gilmore and B. Joseph Pine II wrote a *Harvard Business Review* article, "The Experience Economy," in which they studied the evolution of the way we've bought goods and services over the last century. To illustrate the idea of experience-seeking, Gilmore and Pine came up with an analogy I love: the birthday cake.

If you wanted to make a birthday cake for your sweetheart back in the 1920s, it would have been a laborious process, and price would have been your first consideration. You would have gone to the market to buy flour, eggs, milk, sugar, and baking soda from several vendors. You would have brought your own bag in which to haul everything back to your house. You would have mixed all the ingredients by hand and baked the cake yourself. That's the way we made cakes—and bought goods and services—in the early part of the 20th century.

The next stage was the 1940s to the 1970s, when you could buy everything for a birthday cake synthesized in one neat box. Betty Crocker put it all together for you: Just dump it in a bowl, add water, stir it up, pop it in the oven and there you go—instant birthday cake. This was the beginning of outsourcing.

Then there were the 1980s, when things changed even more. People were opening bakeries and stores like Carvel in which you could buy all sorts of ready-made cakes. If you wanted to celebrate a birthday, not only did you outsource the effort of synthesizing the goods and the materials, you actually outsourced the cooking process. All you had to do was order it and pick it up.

In the 1990s, you had more options than ever before. You could not only outsource the making of the cake, you could also outsource the entire birthday experience. One of the most popular places for this was Chuck E. Cheese's. Now you've got games to play and a show to watch, and not only did they bake the cake and bring it out to you, they also gave you balloons, food, and drinks, and they sent people to your table to sing to you. All you had to do was show up and have fun.

The birthday cake has continued to evolve. It's not even about the actual birthday cake anymore; it's about how unique and remarkable you can make it. You can now buy cakes that walk and talk. You can get one that is an exact replica of your face, your house, your car—whatever floats your boat. If you don't know what I'm talking about, spend an evening watching the Food Network.

In summary, when you think about what's happened to the evolution of the birthday cake over the last hundred years, our expectations have gone from *Give me the goods*, to *Synthesize it*, to *Cook it for me*, to *Give me an experience*, to *Make it remarkable*.

That's what customers are looking for today: remarkable experiences. The irony is that we want it to be unique every time. That means that nothing is ever good enough from a business perspective. Take a look at these eye-opening statistics from the 2010 North America Customer Experience Impact Report[17]:

- 85 percent of respondents say they'd be willing to pay up to 25 percent more to ensure a superior customer experience.
- 55 percent became a customer of a company because of its reputation for great customer service.
- 55 percent are willing to recommend a company because of outstanding service, more so than product or price.
- 66 percent cited customer service as the biggest driver for encouraging greater spending.
- 82 percent have stopped doing business with an organization because of a poor customer experience.
- 95 percent have taken action as a result of a negative experience.
- 79 percent told others about a negative experience.

It's mind-blowing to me that even in this heightened recession, 85 percent of people polled said they would pay more for a remarkable

---

17 RightNow Technologies, "Customer Experience Impact Report 2010," 9 Oct. 2010, accessed 6 Oct. 2011, http://www.slideshare.net/RightNow/2010-customer-experience-impact.

experience. It's also interesting that eight in ten people would leave and not come back if they had a bad experience. So, exceeding customer expectations is the new standard. Exceeding expectations generally means that you're doing some of the little things right. It doesn't mean you're giving stuff away or offering big discounts. It just means you have gone beyond the customer's baseline expectations.

One company that does this well is American Express. I have a business account there, and they call me twice each year just to touch base. The first time it happened, I was confused.

"Mr. Mechlinski, this is American Express. How's everything going?"

"Great," I replied. "What can I do for you today?"

"We're calling to check in to see how your business is doing these days."

"Ummm . . . okay. Seriously, you can just come right out and tell me what you want. I do this for a living, you know."

"No, you don't understand. We're just calling to say hello and see how your company is doing. That's all, really."

Wow. With one little phone call, American Express made itself noteworthy to me. Suddenly, I'm talking about them in a positive way, and once I start doing that, it's like lightning in a bottle. I become an evangelist. I go on Facebook later and tell everybody how great they are. The power of word-of-mouth marketing has been around forever, but it has been amplified because of the Internet. It's also amplified because we're in a less trusting economy.

What's great about this philosophy is that anyone can do it. It doesn't matter if you're a solo entrepreneur or the CEO of a global company. Even so, few companies seem to get it. If a company of any size wants to grow regardless, this is the mindset they *must* adopt. When you show your customers you are willing to do whatever it takes to help *them* be successful, your company will grow.

The Process

The process is simple: Ask questions, listen, and then do something about it. There are four straightforward actions you can begin doing today to put yourself, your people, and your organization on the road to providing remarkable experiences for your customers:

- Express your gratitude to your customers
- Recommend your customers
- Educate your customers
- Become involved in your customers' worlds

The first is one of the most basic things you learned in preschool, yet it's one of the most profound contributors to your success in life: saying *thank you* when someone does something nice for you.

When was the last time you expressed your **gratitude** to a client beyond a halfhearted "thanks" as they headed out the door? When was the last time a business owner stopped to thank you for your patronage? Random acts of gratitude don't happen often enough in business. Whether you say it out loud, express it in a handwritten note, or send a box of fruit, a sincere expression of gratitude has a huge and immediate impact on your customers because it is so rare. You want to become noteworthy? *Say thank you.*

The next time somebody visits your office, stop what you're doing, look them in the eye, shake their hand and say, "Listen, I want to thank you for your business. Thank you for your faith and your trust in us. I know you've got a lot of options, and we're all so grateful you picked us."

Making that kind of personal connection with your client is something neither one of you will soon forget.

The second remarkable thing you can do is **recommend** their company. Get to know them well and learn their business inside out. Then, write a personal recommendation on their LinkedIn profile. Give them a good grade on Yelp or one of the other online rating sites. Write them a reference letter. You could recommend their product or services to someone else, meaning you actually go out and find them more business. Become an external sales force for them. They'll soon begin to see you as a trusted advisor and a true partner, someone who doesn't just advocate for them but who's willing to drive the relationships that create more value for them within your shared network.

The third one is a personal favorite of mine because it's so much fun: **Educate** your clients. Do you have a specific niche of information that would help your clients on an ongoing basis? Share it. You could send them an article you wrote, a link to your blog, or a video your company put together. You could create a monthly or yearly webinar for your clients. It doesn't have to be information from your company; maybe you came across something from an outside source that might be helpful to them: a white paper about the latest trends or a video about something notable in their industry.

Keep in mind that you're educating your clients not because you're trying to sell them a new product or service, but because you're sincerely trying to help them gain expertise and become stronger. You're educating them because a rising tide lifts all boats.

The final thing you can do to give a remarkable experience is to **participate** in your client's world. Go to events that matter to them: their client appreciation events, ceremonies where they're receiving an award, webinars or conferences they're hosting. Maybe your client is passionate about Big Brothers Big Sisters and they're holding a fundraising event. Volunteer to help. Maybe they're sponsoring a Little League team that's in the championship game. Go sit in the stands and cheer them on. Be an active supporter. Obviously, participation is the most time-intensive way to provide a remarkable experience for a customer. It is undoubtedly over the top. But it is the one that says it all, because it's not just me hearing what you say; it's me taking the time to watch what you do and how you do it. It's me valuing you so much that I'm willing to make time stand still just for you.

Why must you go to these extremes to thank, advocate, educate and actively participate with your clients? Because the leaders of every other company in the world are having the exact same conversation among themselves that you and I are having right now, and if they're not, they're going to be out of business very soon. They're asking themselves how to keep the clients they have and how to get even more. That's the buzz that everyone is talking about. So if every company is having this conversation, the question becomes: *What are you going to do to make yourself stand out?*

What are you going to do to distinguish yourself from the rest of the pack? Short of having lots of cash to buy your clients a luxury suite at a sporting event or send them on a trip to Bermuda, what can you do to make doing business with your company a remarkable experience?

Because, typically, what's remarkable in a client's eyes has nothing to do with how much money you spend and everything to do with how much *effort* you spend and how compelling a story you tell.

Tell that story. Make that effort. You, your clients, and the GDP will be darn glad you did.

The Client Experience in Practice:
Oliver Carr and Carr Workplaces

Washington, DC-based Carr Workplaces provides office space to independent work groups and professionals—not just any office space, but extraordinary working environments. With emphasis on outstanding customer service, the company strives to create professional spaces that build community among the people who work there. Chief Executive Officer Oliver Carr, together with Chief Operating Officer Angie O'Grady, explain how the company's innovation and attention to detail have enabled it to grow.

Joe: Give me the history. I love your story, even before Carr Workplaces.

Oliver: The history of our company is that I was a homebuilder post-World War II. After that, I started in the commercial office, hotel, and residential building business in the city of Washington, DC. As our company became larger in the office-building world, I realized that most small users of office space were not treated very well. They were stuck in a corner, in the least desirable office space and they were not considered important. The brokerage community did not take them seriously. So they did not receive much respect. After our real estate company went public and become a national company, we acquired HQ, an executive suite company. At that time, it was the world's largest executive suite provider with more than

400 centers. In early 2000, it was necessary to sell HQ because it did not conform to the income standards for a real estate investment trust (REIT). So with some reluctance, we did part with it. As it turns out, HQ later found itself in some serious financial trouble, its new owner, Blackstone, went into bankruptcy and HQ was acquired again, this time by Regus, now the global leader in our sector. So our old company represents about half of Regus' company and most of the American coverage that it has.

After HQ was sold to Blackstone, it seemed that there was an opportunity for us to reinvent ourselves with particular interest in the small business professional that we had witnessed as being not too well handled in the past. So Carr Workplaces was formed. Its leader, Angie O'Grady, was a former employee of HQ and knew the business well. At the time, I was fascinated by the fact that two-thirds of the job growth of the country was (and has always been) with small business. So, not only was the real estate industry ignoring the small business person as such, but it was ignoring the growth that they produced. I thought on both counts it looked like a real opportunity. Over the years, we have grown Carr Workplaces to the point where we have national coverage in a modest way. We're in ten different states and have more than thirty-five centers. Our plans are to continue to grow, more rapidly now and create dense coverage nationwide. Among our client base are corporate users who are multimarket users, and while they make up just a small fraction of our client base, they are an important element of it. They are best served by having deeper national coverage. We have found that the small users typically have a more "regional" need, but it is our goal to serve both multimarket and small users in as many markets as possible. We are on a mission to create extraordinary workplaces for everyone with a particular emphasis on small business because they are so important to our country's economic health.

We knew that most of the small business professionals were in gloomy spaces that looked like the General Services Administration reincarnated. Any shade of gray would work. Lights weren't important, color was absolutely unessential. So we looked at the psychology of color and we retained the services of a small architectural firm in Alexandria, Virginia. We thought to introduce color, a sense of energy and light to the centers would be a good idea. So we started with the place and then great people. Our standards for employees are high—in addition to being adequately suited for the job; they must also be bright, warm, and engaging. I used Enterprise, the car company, as a model for that. I rent a car at Enterprise not because the car is any better or I get more gas mileage, but because I love the way I'm received by their people. We're intent on having great people, as well as a great place physically. Our team members are enriching the services provided to the small business or independent workers that use our office space.

In addition, as we open centers in cities across the county, we have developed an interest in the children being left behind. They have all too often been deprived of the opportunity to flourish because of the lack of nurturing—broken families, lack of nutrition, and the underlying educational climate in their schools. If we can help some of them by availing them of resources that can help them succeed in school, we feel deeply rewarded. So the notion is that as we build the number of our centers, each time we open one, we will help open the mind of a child so they too can grow into young entrepreneurs who will succeed independently. The folks who work from our centers are largely independents. Our hope is to deepen their experience as a community, so they can also grow by exchanging ideas and working together, thus creating a launch pad for the local economy.

Joe: It's funny that you bring up Enterprise. One of the inspirations for our growth methodology is that a company needs a story. This concept was given to me by the gentleman at the last house I ever painted, Stan Burns. Stan was a banker, but he had a passion for writing and he wrote the Enterprise Rent-A-Car story. For the last twenty years, every time a new person gets hired, they have to read this book. Enterprise wanted them to understand who the company was.

People will read this and say, "I get it, customer service is supposed to be important." Then we have examples like Starbucks or Southwest or Enterprise, and people leap to, "They're big companies and they can afford to do it." What gave you the inspiration or the confidence that out of the gate, a company could start with the client in mind?

Oliver: I've always noticed that people need community. The first office I ever had when I was a homebuilder was over a hardware store in Rockville, Maryland. I was alone, just me and the mice, so I appreciate the fact that being alone literally in your workplace is not a good feeling. Working in isolation in some vast office building or in a small structure isn't productive but being part of a community of peers, of other independent business professionals, makes employees feel better and increases their productivity. So the community part was really important me, from the beginning.

Secondly, it was apparent to us there were certain services and places many of our clients could not afford alone. For example, they really could not afford the conferencing space they occasionally need or the community café. I also think it's important for people to have an aim that's higher than their own short-term one. For them to be identified as doing "good" in the overall community is important to them. We want to have our clients feel like they are part of a team even though they are operating independently within it—give them their own identity, their own recognition for their activities and enterprise, but not to feel alone in the world, and it seems to work.

Joe: Why don't you think more companies choose the path that you have chosen?

Oliver: Every now and then in every activity, every industry, you can find inefficiencies or oversights. I've been very aware of this for twenty years and finally decided to do something about it. We routinely receive bios of clients in centers from all over the country. It is fascinating what you learn about our clients when you sit down and quietly read their bio. You realize, this person plays golf, this one is a swimmer, or he plays the violin, or he's a great reader. His or her vocation may be accounting or it may be in a science. The huge variety of both interests and capabilities is fascinating. Almost all consistently say they really want to do something for someone else. They want to help in their communities and that is reassuring.

Joe: As you went from one center to thirty-five centers, what were some of the biggest challenges around continuing to elevate the client experience as top of mind for everyone? When you hired Angie as employee number one, it was probably easy, because she had a lot of the things you looked at as ideal, but as you've grown your organization to 120 employees, what have been some of the challenges of keeping that consistent?

Oliver: We grew rather slowly and therefore Angie was able to carefully and personally select the key person, the General Manager, for each center. Angie made sure that person was able to engage with clients, to empathize with them, to "look them in the eye," and give them a smile in the morning, even if it was a before the first cup of coffee. So that part of growing the business and making sure we had the right team in place was not too difficult, but when we acquired a small company in 2009 we had a whole new set of team members—team members who had not been hand selected by Angie. It threw us off course for a while. So really, the only bump we've had in our growth was in assimilating those team members. Moving forward, we hope to acquire other companies, but recognize that is problematic. It is easier to grow your own, but we're confident our culture is one that other teams can embrace.

Joe: If you had to give someone who was starting out in a different industry a playbook of lessons that you learned over the last ten-plus years, what would be some of the major lessons about growth, customer service or client experience?

Oliver: There's risk to growth. You make some mistakes, but that's how you learn. I find it a little difficult answering your question because my whole life has been entrepreneurial. Nothing is easy. If it's easy, it's not fun. I think we really experienced nothing that surprised us, but you have to recognize the fact that as you grow, you will do some things that you wish you had not done, but that's how you learn to grow better. I'm sure Enterprise has done certain things they later corrected and they've become better, in their people selection, training process—the same with us. My real response to that question is just to go do it and learn by doing it. Do not hold back and try to figure it all out, because that's not possible. Put your toe in the water. You can only get slightly burned.

Joe: Some of the things you mentioned in the beginning were key to looking at how the market was treating the small business, things like brightening up the office, designing it in a way that allowed for community. What are other examples that you thought were key around client experience?

Oliver: We are constantly working to evolve and improve the experience of our clients. At the forefront of this, are our team members. With a lean team supporting our clients and center, it is imperative that all team members feel valued for what they do each day and how it can positively (or negatively) impact our business and our clients' experience. For example, I think the people at the reception desk play a key role in how a person feels when he or she walks into any office environment. This goes back to Enterprise. The Enterprise experience to me—I'm entirely indifferent to how much gas is needed to fill the tank but when the auto rental company can offer eye contact and an intelligent conversation, that is the key.

Joe: If I'm not mistaken, the front desk person is called the Director of First Impression.

Oliver: Not anymore.

Joe: Why did you make that switch?

Angie: The feedback we got from our team, and we do try to listen to our team, is that for them, it felt like the title said that the only thing we cared about was their smiling pretty face as opposed to the services they were truly providing. So they felt like while, at first glance it had a great tone and meaning to it, the receptionist team didn't feel like it was descriptive enough in terms of the whole breadth of services they were offering. So we now call our front desk team our Client Services Associates which focuses on all of the services they are offering to our clients each day.

Joe: One of the things we talk about in our methodology is that way you treat your employees is very indicative of how they will treat your customers. So that was just a small change in your mind, but a big change in their eyes. So imagine now in their minds, they are there with this deeper level of responsibility, this altruistic "I'm here to serve," not just answer the phone and smile, which is great.

Oliver: To follow through on that point, most of the folks who work all through the company are college graduates. If you major in philosophy and then you have to sit there and answer the phone all day and that's all you do that does not portend well for the future... I think a challenge going forward, and what we're continuing to address, is how to deepen and enrich the work experience so that person is engaged in understanding each client and the different needs of each client. So we want people to be engaged because we recognize that makes them happy and productive.

Joe: How do you keep everybody excited?

Oliver: Most people like being in companies in which there is upward mobility, and we intend to maintain this by growing. The last time I was at Enterprise, I asked this young lady who told me all about the training program. She said, "It's a great private company. I like it because I can move up. I don't like being here so much doing this, but I can move up." We want the same feeling.

Joe: They went as far as, back in the late 1990s, calling it a management training program. I think Southwest Airlines learned a lot from what they did in hiring college grads for what looked like pretty menial jobs at the end of the day.

Oliver: By the way, we do something quite romantic every year. We pick a star of the year, and the star of the year gets a trip with a companion to Paris. We want to really recognize the star when we have one. We pick our star based on a number of criteria, but their ability to create a client "community" is right up at the top.

Joe: Anything else that has been crucial to your success in business?

Oliver: What's true of Enterprise and it's true of us. It's all about the people, both the people who work in it and the people we serve. I call it capitalism with a small c.

Joe: At the end of the day, what do you want the company to be known for?

Oliver: I'd love it to be a company just as, Pan Am was at one time, a place where young people wanted to work because it was an exciting place to be. I want the same thing for this company. The more it can extend its reach and support the healthy growth of small independent entrepreneurs and professionals, to me that is beneficial to society and will help many young people gain valuable experience.

Angie: Talking about the sense of community, one of the great things we've found over time is that our clients think that they're here and it's such a great place, and then they start realizing they have friends who work for small companies and then they refer those people so they can in turn create an environment for themselves in which they're surrounding themselves with like-minded individuals. That is a fabulous way for us to grow, because typically when a client refers us to someone, we close that opportunity. And again, it creates that reason for them to all want to stay here—they can't leave because they'll have to leave their friend "Bob" behind. So it just creates this incredible community that is sticky and clients stay for a long time, not just because of us, but because of the people they're working with, which is what we're ultimately trying to create.

Oliver: The energy really is theirs, not ours. Some centers you marvel at when you walk in. They can be quite different. The one on Park Avenue in New York is different from the one in Alexandria, Virginia. When you walk in and a client takes you down the hall and introduces you to their friend it gives you a warm feeling. They create their own sense of place, relationships and energy and that's terrific.

Joe: When you think about growing, particularly with the difference between the local service provider and the national company that just needs more options to put its people, do you see word-of-mouth still being a big part of growth as it becomes more national?

Oliver: Absolutely. What's interesting with the corporate road warriors is they also like a home. When the big guy says, "Go wherever you want, but you've got to be in Washington every Thursday," the road warrior is happier if they don't land in some isolated box, but go to a real "home" with other folks.

Angie: That's an important notion, too, when we're talking about the independent professional, it's not necessarily just the entrepreneur. It could be that person who works for Microsoft or Google, but they are the one or two people who just happen to be stationed in Old Town, Alexandria. They still need that community because they're away from the corporate office and their peers and team members from their company.

Oliver: From the mother company's point of view, it's great. It's very efficient for them to use our services. As we continue to grow, we are focused on ensuring that we have a foundation in place to support the centers and the team. We have to perform well every time we open a center so it is essential that we have processes in place that support all efforts at the center level. These include not just the processes themselves but the right leadership team at the corporate level. It's easy to open a center, but if the support team is not functioning well, that's not a very happy situation. We are working on perfecting the center and improving and strengthening the corporate support team at home.

Exercise: Planting the Seeds for Growth through Client Experience

To understand the effectiveness of your client experience strategy, answer the following questions by checking the box under the most accurate answer.

Question	Strongly Agree	Agree	Somewhat Agree	Somewhat Disagree	Disagree	Strongly Disagree
1. We regularly receive unsolicited referrals from our client base.						
2. If we were to survey our clients, they would describe our service and the relationship as remarkable.						
3. One of our core values and/or main initiatives is focused on the client experience we provide.						
4. Our team proactively discusses ways to over-service our clients.						
5. We rarely lose our clients to our competition.						
6. Our employees across the board would consistently describe what a remarkable client experience is.						

Question	Strongly Agree	Agree	Somewhat Agree	Somewhat Disagree	Disagree	Strongly Disagree
7. I personally show gratitude to our clients on a regular basis.						
8. I personally recommend my clients to others through word-of-mouth and social media on a regular basis.						
9. I personally educate my clients by sending articles of interest, blogs, white papers, etc. on a regular basis.						
10. In the last month, I attended an event that was of interest to one of my clients.						

The first six questions are based on the overall client experience you think your organization provides, while the next four relate to your leadership in delivering a remarkable client experience. Delivering this experience can become the foundation for your culture, but it starts with you. If you rated any questions as anything other than "Agree" or "Strongly Agree," dive deeper into those questions and ask "why." For an immediate impact, we recommend:

- Make a commitment to showing gratitude to at least one client per week.
- Make a commitment to recommending at least one client per week.
- Make a commitment to educating at least one client per week.

- Make a commitment to getting involved in the world of one client per month (attending an event, showing support, etc.).

Additional Resources

For more ways to plant the seeds for growth through Client Experience, visit www.growregardless.com/book/clientexp for a free training video.

Chapter 8

SUIT UP
OR SHUT UP

*You are never given a wish without also being given the power
to make it come true. You may have to work for it, however.*
—**Richard Bach**

Throughout this book, I've given a detailed roadmap for how a company or an organization can grow regardless, but what it really comes down to is individuals stepping forward and being the best they can be no matter what their circumstances. When I think about that theme, the person who lives up to it the most in my mind is my father, Jim.

Look up the word "grit" in the dictionary and you'll see a picture of my dad. Jim Mechlinski is the quintessential baby boomer blue-collar worker. He was born and raised in Baltimore, and his childhood makes mine look like a trip to Disneyland. My father never knew his biological father. His mother remarried four or five times, twice to the same guy. Despite being wicked smart, my dad never earned a college degree.

One day in 1975, my dad, who was 19 at the time, was driving along and saw a cute girl hitchhiking on the side of the road. He picked her up, and one thing led to another. The girl, who had dreams of becoming an actress, left for California shortly thereafter, but as soon as she got there she discovered she was pregnant. With me.

So Mom (and I, *in utero*) returned to Baltimore. She and Dad got married in September, much to the chagrin of her father and my dad's parents, all of whom saw disaster written all over this thing. I was born three months later. Up to that point, my dad had been knocking around, probably even doing some things he shouldn't have been doing (according to him). But the second he found out he was having a kid and getting married, something inside him shifted. He became determined to be the best provider he could possibly be for his little family. One of his buddies worked at a warehouse, and Dad went there as soon as he heard there was an opening. When the boss asked him why he was looking for a job, Dad explained that his wife was pregnant with their first baby and he needed to work so he could take proper care of them.

"I can only promise you eight hours' pay for an honest day's work," said the boss.

"You'll never have anybody work as hard for you as I will," Dad replied.

The boss looked my dad in the eye and said, "Son, you go home and tell your wife that everything's going to be okay."

So it was that Dad was hired as a forklift operator in that warehouse. Every morning at five o'clock he got up, pulled on his overalls and went to work, usually putting in twelve- or thirteen-hour days. It was bitter cold in the wintertime and sweltering hot in the summer, but he never complained. I never once heard him talk about how tired he was or how hard he had to work. He just kept going day after day, fueled by his determination to do a good job and to provide his family with the two things he never had growing up—stability and security.

About seventeen years into his tenure with the company, the boss sold the warehouse. Lots of guys lost their jobs as a result of that transaction, but my dad was not one of them. The boss took Dad and five other men with him, stuck them in a little trailer, called it their office and put them to work launching his next business: a trucking company. My dad recalls that all six guys couldn't stand up in the trailer at the same time because there wasn't enough room. They started with a couple dozen trucks and worked tirelessly to build the company from there.

Today, thirty-five years after he first put on a pair of overalls and started driving a forklift in that dusty warehouse, I am proud to say that my dad is now vice president of operations and one of many partners in that highly successful trucking company with a fleet of more than 1,400 trucks and as many employees, if not more.

What's the lesson from Dad's story? It's this:

Working at something for thirty-five years might seem entirely too daunting, exhausting, and unrealistic, especially if you've not had excellent role models to light your way.

Becoming a leader might seem impossible, especially if you aren't formally trained for it.

Being able to keep your word and maintain your integrity might seem like a pipe dream, especially since no one can predict the obstacles and events that might arise to try to sabotage that worthy goal.

But in the end, you can still grow regardless. My father is living proof.

Dad used to wear overalls to drive a forklift. Now he wears business casual to help drive a robust, profitable company. He is the personification of "Suit up or shut up." He also happens to be my hero and one of the most honorable people I have ever known.

Small to midsize companies have huge learning opportunities before us: *We are in this together, but we need to go at this alone.* The private sector must step up and provide the vision, leadership, and urgency our nation needs right now. Hopefully, our entrepreneurial mindset of "always finding a way" will spill over to those members of our working population who truly need it to do their jobs successfully. Can you imagine the progress we would make if all of us were to practice **The eQ Growth Methodology** and lead by example, living out our own core values and those of our companies?

To me, the entrepreneurial mindset has three practical components that we leaders can promote to help our teams, our clients, and our communities to grow regardless, and they are three of the most valuable lessons I learned from my dad. They are:

1. Hustle
2. Heart
3. Humility

Hustle is simple. It's not about putting in more time; it's about more *focused time*. Hustle is your pace, your energy. It's constantly looking for the edge of improvement. It's the feeling that you don't *have* to do this, you *get* to do this. Entrepreneurs like Thomas Edison, Walt Disney, Colonel Harland Sanders of Kentucky Fried Chicken fame, Bill Hewlett, and Dave Packard all knew the power of hustle. These men didn't let the difficult economies of their day stop them from launching and growing successful companies. They simply put their heads down and pushed their way through without giving up.

While hustle speaks to stamina, heart speaks to intensity. Heart is the passion and persistence with which you live your life and do your work. The title character in the classic movie *Rudy* had heart. He was undersized and outmatched, yet he found a way to live out his passion for the game of football. Heart is also about "having a heart"—liking people, being compassionate toward your fellow human beings, being sympathetic, and realizing how we're all connected. We are not isolated from other people's problems. We can't grow unless we acknowledge, and act upon, that truth.

Finally, there is humility. We leaders must try our best to never believe that we have arrived, we are good enough, and we have no more to learn. Our humility is the anchor of our Leader-Ship. Charles Haddon Spurgeon once said, "Humility is to make a *right* estimate of one's self." The right estimate is not the low estimate or the high estimate. It's the true estimate. There's great comfort in being humble, in understanding that you have much more learning and growing to do, in recognizing what you're *not* good at, and in turning your attention away from yourself and watching the amazing things around you.

But, as Malcolm Forbes said, "Too many people overvalue what they are not and undervalue what they are." You cannot claim something you are not, but you certainly should claim what you have earned. For example, our resident number-cruncher at entreQuest did a financial analysis of our company and found that our growth rate was in the 91st percentile of all management consulting companies under $10 million in revenue from 2010 to 2011. I took that startling information to my people and asked, "What would we do differently if we knew we were in the top ten percent of management consulting firms in the country?" We decided we'd probably stop seeing our small stature as a disadvantage. We decided that it's time to own our space, to continue working hard and smart, and to be exactly who we are.

I suggest you do the same.

To inspire that mindset, I share this poem by Marianne Williamson:

> **Our Deepest Fear**
> *Our deepest fear is not that we are inadequate.*
> *Our deepest fear*
> *is that we are powerful beyond measure.*
> *It is our light, not our darkness,*
> *that most frightens us.*
> *We ask ourselves, who am I to be brilliant, gorgeous,*
> *talented and fabulous? Actually who are we **NOT** to be?*
> *You are a child of God.*
> *Your playing small doesn't serve the world.*[18]

To acknowledge our power and use it with compassion, to leave the world a bit better, to redeem a social condition, to live in a way that makes another person's life easier . . . that's pretty powerful stuff. But it's the right stuff, and it's what will restore America's financial vitality and morale. Private-sector leaders have proven their resourcefulness up to this point, but there is so much more we can do.

We are all in this together, but we need to go at this alone. We cannot stand idly by and waste another minute expecting our government to bail us out, or get out of our way, or intervene on our behalf, or cut our taxes . . . or whatever it is that each of us thinks our government ought to be

---

18 Marianne Williamson, *A Return to Love: Reflections on the Principles of a Course in Miracles*, New York: HarperCollins, 1992, 190–191.

doing. We don't have time to wait. Instead, let us recover our core values and summon the hustle, heart and humility to best serve our country. Let us move forward one by one, with each of us remembering our own individual *whys*, sharing our stories, treating other people as our greatest assets, keeping our word, resetting ourselves and our organizations swiftly and surely whenever necessary, and expressing gratitude for all the goodness in our lives. In other words, let us suit up or shut up. There is no room for excuses in our new-new reality. You now have all the tools you need to begin rebuilding yourself, your team, your company, and our country. Start using them today, right now.

Then, pass this book on to another business leader, and another. Pass it on to ten people. If only two of those ten people actually read it, practice it, and hire ten new workers as a result, you'll have the satisfaction of knowing that you helped to get twenty people employed, that you personally did something meaningful toward getting our country back on track. What better way to live out this book's theme of growing regardless?

Finally, as you go about this important work, remember: On the path that leads to growth, the only thing that will ever stand between you and the success you seek . . . is you.

Step up to this worthy challenge, and let's all grow regardless.

Acknowledgements— Attitude of Gratitude

THIS PART OF THE book is simultaneously the most fun and the most challenging. It's fun because it gives me the chance to express my gratitude for all the people who have helped me along the way, even outside the realm of this book. It's also a challenge because I don't want to leave anyone out. Please bear with me as I honor the people who have lent me a hand and helped me grow regardless.

To my parents: This book's dedication is trivial compared to all you have sacrificed and all you have taught me. By showing me firsthand the difference between right and wrong, the meaning of hard work, how to be a good person, how to appreciate the small things and how to never take for granted what we have, you are the ones who set the foundation for who I am today. Mom, Dad and Rose, you are truly the best three parents I could have asked for. *Grow Regardless* is a testament to your loving care in teaching me how to live a good, honest life.

To my family: My wife Erica, my daughter Eliana (Ellie), and my newborn son, James. If my parents are why I am here, then you are the reason I get up every morning and do my best to carry on their great example. You are my inspiration. I think this book is so important to me because I want to make sure that my daughter and son have the same opportunities in this country that I did. Every good thing I will ever do is because of you. I love you.

I include my in-laws, Jim and Mickey, because you also offer support, strength and example. Thank you for your support! We are in this together!

To the rest of my family: The list of names goes on forever, and so does my thanks to all of you. You helped me through the passing of my mother, gave me support when I was in college, helped feed me when I was hungry, gave me money when I was broke, lifted my spirits when I was down. You were always my #1 fans, and just knowing you were there meant more to me than you can ever imagine. I couldn't ask for a better support structure than I've had. You all know who you are.

There are two more people who mean the world to me: Misti Aaronson and Jeremy Steinberg, my current partners at entreQuest. If I had to pick two people out of all the leaders I've worked with over the last eleven years who have stuck with me, had my back and fully lived the values, mission and purpose of entreQuest, it would be you. Your work ethic is above reproach. Misti, your selflessness and grit keep us on track and always moving forward. Jeremy, your energy and heart challenge me to reach higher every day. I can't predict the future, but I can say without a doubt that with you two beside me, the sky is the limit.

The next acknowledgement is special. It's to my good friend, and co-founder of entreQuest, Jason Pappas. You have certainly filled a starring role in my journey. We've been through the war together and shared all of the ups and downs. Thanks for always being there both personally and professionally.

This book highlights five remarkable leaders: Doug Beigel, David Zdrojewski, John Walden, Chris Krause, and Mr. Oliver Carr. Your willingness to let me share your stories, highlight your journeys and share your accomplishments is what makes this book real. Thank you again.

I want to thank every client, employee, prospect, and competitor we've ever worked with for showing us firsthand how companies can grow regardless. We've learned from every one of you. You've all played a huge role in our growth and development, and I hope you're as appreciative as I am of our time together.

A special thank you goes to Annie O'Dell. Although you're no longer with us, you will always live on in my heart, because I remember the words you taught me: Love never dies, and goodness always prevails.

To Pamela Suárez, my partner in crime who helped make this book what it is, thank you so much for showing me the way. Calling you simply a writer does not do you justice. Hopefully, this is only the first of many books we'll make together.

To my editor Amy Burroughs, you rock! You have been patient with me throughout this process. You are a true talent. Thank you.

And finally, there were others who played a huge part in my life and in my journey in writing this book, running a successful company, and being the lucky guy I am today. These are people who may never even read this book, people who likely didn't think of themselves as mentors to me, but who played a significant role in teaching me the way: Stan Burns, Coach Roger Wrenn, Steve Lishansky, Coach Jim Margraff, Robert Butler, Harry Watkins, Joe Cowan, Chris Gaito, Coach Tony Pasco . . . and the list goes on. My gratitude to you is boundless.

ABOUT THE AUTHOR

*"Hard work and integrity are at the foundation
of the company he co-founded. . ."*
—Baltimore Business Journal

Joe Mechlinski is a man with a mission: to make a difference by giving voice to America's small to midsize business leaders and teaching them how to grow their organizations regardless of their size, their industry and the economy. Joe is the award-winning co-founder and CEO of entreQuest, Inc., a Baltimore consulting firm that has helped hundreds of companies prosper through some of the worst economic times in American history.

Recognized as a national authority on U.S. small business growth, Joe is a popular speaker, webinar host, author, and business columnist. His company has been featured in *Entrepreneur, The Wall Street Journal Online, The (Maryland) Daily Record,* and the *Baltimore Business Journal,* which named entreQuest one of its "Best Places to Work" in 2011 and 2012. Joe has also been recognized as a Very Important Professional in 2010 and a Most Admired CEO in 2012 by *The (Maryland) Daily Record.* The Maryland Chamber of Commerce chose entreQuest as its Small Business of the Year in 2004. Recently, Mechlinski was invited to be part of the

Employee Happiness blog site and is one of twenty-six world-renowned authors committed to sharing tips to improve the employee experience.

Joe grew up in inner-city Baltimore, where he learned what it's like to be undervalued and underserved. But he also experienced firsthand the powerful effect that education and mentors can have on a young person's life. After graduating from a high school with one of the worst graduation rates in the state and being named Maryland's 1995 Scholar Athlete by the National Football Foundation and College Hall of Fame, Joe was recruited by Johns Hopkins University, where he played football and earned a bachelor's degree in economics—while working at least one part-time job (and sometimes as many as three at a time) in small businesses around campus.

These experiences in our small business economy led Joe to his distinctive business philosophy, centered on the notion that relationships matter and people are always a company's greatest asset. With that philosophy as his foundation, Joe co-founded a lead generation company, a sales and marketing firm, and an entrepreneurial development company that grew to more than 100 employees in three years. In 2000, Joe co-founded entreQuest at the age of twenty-three. Within five years, he built it into a thriving multi-million-dollar consulting practice that continues to grow.

Joe's civic involvement reflects his passion for education and mentorship. He co-founded the b4students Foundation, which links corporate mentors with at-risk students for their entire high-school careers, and he is a board member for Big Brothers Big Sisters of Central Maryland. Past board memberships include the League for People with Disabilities, Baltimore Urban Debate League, National Football Foundation and College Hall of Fame–Greater Baltimore Chapter, and Johns Hopkins University Alumni Executive Committee. He is also a graduate of the Greater Baltimore Committee's 2007 Leadership program.

Joe is a voracious reader and has read more than 400 books on business, sales, self-improvement, marketing, and history. He also survived a trek up Mount Kilimanjaro and his first (and last) marathon in Baltimore.

FEATURED COMPANIES

Carr Workplaces

At Carr Workplaces, we are proud of our heritage, and for a relatively young company we have a lot of it. Founded in 2003 by Oliver T. Carr, Jr., we are the culmination of decades of experience in commercial real estate services and development. The following is a quick synopsis of our storied past.

Mr. Carr founded The Oliver Carr Company in 1962 and built it into the most active commercial development firm in DC. Then in 1993, the Carr Company became CarrAmerica, a NYSE-traded real estate investment trust. In addition to being a leading owner and developer of commercial real estate, CarrAmerica was the largest owner and operator of business centers throughout the United States. The company was sold in 2006 to affiliates of The Blackstone Group.

That brings us to present day with Carr Workplaces continuing the long legacy of forward-looking Carr-family innovation by creating extraordinary office environments that deliver flexibility and value for independent work groups and professionals.

For more information about Carr Workplaces, please visit them online at http://carrworkplaces.com.

COLA

COLA was founded in 1988 as a private alternative to help laboratories stay in compliance with the new Clinical Laboratory Improvement Amendments (CLIA). COLA is the largest accreditor in the U.S. accrediting approximately 8,000 medical laboratories and provides the clinical laboratory with a program of education, consultation, and accreditation. The organization is an independent, non-profit accreditor whose education program and standards enable clinical laboratories and staff to meet U.S. CLIA and other regulatory requirements. COLA's program is endorsed by the American Medical Association (AMA), American Academy of Family Practitioners (AAFP), American College of Physicians (ACP) and the Joint Commission on Accreditation of Healthcare Organizations (TJC) also recognizes COLA's laboratory accreditation program. COLA is committed to helping laboratories achieve excellence in health care by offering a range of services that take the complexity out of accreditation. COLA's goal is simple – to use education and innovative processes to help improve laboratory medicine and patient care.

For more information about COLA, please visit them online at http://cola.org.

National Collegiate Scouting Association (NCSA)

NCSA is a team of 300 former athletes. Our passion is using the lessons of sports to help empower student-athletes to succeed and learn. Below is Chris Krause's story of how and why he began NCSA.

Chris is a former high-school and college athlete. As a junior in high school, Chris received interest from more than a hundred collegiate football programs, from Harvard and Notre Dame to Tennessee and Arizona. Chris thought he would be able to select a college. His football coaches and athletic director assured him that he did not need to worry about a thing, but they could not have been more wrong.

Chris's problem was not that the college coaches did not know who he was. Chris was uninformed about how the recruiting process worked. After completing his senior football season, Chris discovered that some of his friends at rival high schools were setting up official visits and receiving offers from some of the same programs that had contacted him. It was at this time he decided to take matters into his own hands, before every college opportunity was gone.

Chris began to call the coaches who had previously sent him letters to see if they were still looking to fill their linebacker positions. Some said they wished he had called them earlier and that he was too late, but in his calls, he discovered that there were some schools that were still looking. They were impressed with his initiative and the fact that Chris, not his mom or dad, was calling, asking the questions, and showing interest. When coaches requested video footage, he was quick to respond and follow up. After these coaches viewed his tape, he received offers for official visits. He prepared himself for official visits and was determined to make a positive first impression.

Chris's determination and hard work paid off. He received and accepted a full scholarship to Vanderbilt University and graduated in four years.

Building on his experience in being recruited to play in the SEC, Chris began assisting student athletes to get recruited and play in colleges best suited for them. Chris founded NCSA in 2000 with a passion to help turn dreams into a reality. Since its inception, NCSA has become the leader in helping match college coaches with qualified high school students.

Currently, Chris is working to help promote his first book, *Athletes Wanted*, and further empowering Student-Athletes.

For more information about NCSA, please visit them online at http://ncsasports.org.

VibrAlign

David Zdrojewski and John Walden

VibrAlign is committed to growth, both in its laser shaft alignment business and in its people.

Founded in 1983, VibrAlign provides value-added, easy-to-use shaft alignment systems and vibration solutions. We offer field services, training, and a range of laser alignment tools backed by superior customer service.

We are proud to be the exclusive US distributor for Fixturlaser alignment systems, including the Fixturlaser XA and Fixturlaser GO series. Our line of highly accurate and easy-to-use alignment tools also includes the Shaft Hog and the Belt Hog sheave alignment tool.

VibrAlign personnel are located in key cities throughout the United States, with experienced service providers on-call. Whatever alignment or vibration problems you face, VibrAlign can help!

For more information about VibrAlign, please visit them online at http://www.vibralign.com.

ADDITIONAL RESOURCES

If you'd like more information about **The eQ Growth Methodology**, visit our Web site at www.entrequest.com/growthmethodology.

If you'd like someone to help you implement any of the concepts in this book, please contact entreQuest by calling 410-276-1186 or visit www.entrequest.com.

The Client Experience in Practice: Bonus Interview

The President and CEO of a Baltimore-based provider of home delivery pet prescription medications and products used The eQ Growth Methodology to fortify the organization's relationship with its clients, thereby pulling the company back from the brink of collapse.

Joe: Given your organization's history with its clients, what assumptions did the company incorrectly make?

President & CEO: Our company's first assumption was that it would be easy to convince veterinarians, at least a certain critical mass of veterinarians, that we had a service that would help them with medical compliance and with the financial piece of their business. That assumption was correct. What was incorrect was not understanding how threatening that might be to a typical practitioner. If pharmacy is 25 percent or 30 percent of their general revenue and we tell them we can do a pharmacy better than they can, that might make logical sense to a business person, but the typical vet is not a business person.

Typical vets are individuals who went to a veterinary school because they like animals. They're very smart, compassionate people. But when you look at the market, you realize that there are 50,000 practicing veterinarians and there are approximately 25,000 animal practices, meaning that one out of every two practicing veterinarians is a business owner. The reality is that there is no formal business training in veterinary school for these folks. They come into owning and managing these businesses not by choice, but because there are few other alternatives. So when we went up to a practitioner and said, "I can do this better than you" or "I can do this more efficiently," we frightened them. We assumed that they all understood profitability, and we were wrong. That was our first challenge to overcome.

The second wrong assumption the company made was that the frontline people in these practices would automatically be on board with our service. You may convince a practice owner that this is good, but the people within the practice—the technicians, the managers, and the folks who are dealing with the customer in the clinic—if they're not bought in to what we're doing, they're not going to utilize our service. And if our service is cumbersome or if it disrupts the workflow in the clinic or doesn't create any additional motivation for those folks to do their jobs well, then we have failed to solve the clinic's business problem.

I guess it all wraps around to this: Ultimately, we assumed that we knew the challenges of the clinics, but we never stopped to ask them. We didn't take the time to ask, what are the problems that need to be solved for you to be more successful? Once we turned on the light and began asking that question, that helped us flip around the relationship with the clinic owner.

Joe: How does a company not do that from the beginning?

President & CEO: This is one of those great entrepreneurial dilemmas. If Steve Jobs had asked people what they wanted in a computer, he never would have gotten to the Macintosh. He had a vision, and his vision was so complete that he knew exactly where to go with it.

This doesn't mean that the first Macs were everything. But Jobs' death has caused people to stop and take a look at how he approached product design. The notion of going to a focus group or something like that to seek out or test ideas made the guy cringe. I mean, no way was he going to do a focus group, because he knew that the group would be limited by what they thought was possible that day, and not inspired by what the actual possibilities might be.

When you are forming a company, when you are trying to visualize where a product or service offering needs to go, there is a fine line between asking people what they want and having a vision of what they need and being able to convince them that they need it. There are many successful business ventures such as Apple in which people did develop and create something on their own, and there are others that asked folks what they needed and then developed along those lines and made that work.

The reality is that there are successful business models that go down each of those paths. So I think you have to peel back the onion a bit and look for some of the keys to success. Some of the keys to success are picking a space that has the capacity to deal with your go-to market share ideas. Part of it has to do with the completeness of execution that you and your enterprise bring to the table. Part of it has to do with your ability to adapt to new information that comes along. Part of it has to do with your ability to guess right or to analyze customer feedback right, and again, all of those things happen on each of those two paths.

You know why a lot of companies don't get it right? Because they weren't built to be as wildly successful as others. And even applying best practices—whether you pick those up by reading a book, talking to a friend, or thinking about historical precedence—just because you applied those practices to your situation doesn't mean that the other pieces are in place to make it work. You have to investigate and figure out the commonalities of successful enterprises, regardless of whether they chose a customer-reactive or customer-anticipating path. What is envisioning versus analyzing what the market is telling you? You have to have clear vision into your path. You have to have a keen sense of timing, a keen sense of urgency.

There must be clarity within the organization for what it is that you're trying to do, what it means when you get there, and how you're going to change and impact the consumer. And you must be able to manage the messaging and the expectations and everything that goes along with it. If everybody on your team is on the same page and if there's a freedom to make things happen, then I think you're set up to succeed.

Joe: When you became CEO of the business, how did you know the client experience was something for you to focus on?

President & CEO: In all fairness, I don't think it was anything more than realizing that we did not have what I would call deep transactional stickiness. We didn't have a high number of really loyal clinics. It didn't take long to see that our business development or sales efforts were yielding very little impact.

It came down to recognizing that we were talking to a group of people who may or may not understand profit and inventory management. There was a bunch of stuff they didn't understand. But if we were to do a better job of figuring out what their needs were and how to communicate with them on their terms, then we'd have a better chance of breaking down the barriers and creating partnerships. It came down to seeing where our weaknesses were and then trying to uncover the root cause of them. The root cause was that our clinics didn't understand the value that we were bringing them.

Joe: How did you arrive at that? Did you use focus groups? Surveys?

President & CEO: We had past data and we created an industry advisory board, a feedback group. We recognized that we weren't doing an effective job of getting company leadership out into the field to talk to clinics. So we did that, both out in the field and on the phone. We picked up the transactional velocity and gained an understanding of what was going through the consumers' minds relative to using our system. We saw pretty early on that we needed to get back to simplicity. We needed to do a better job of messaging who we were, what we were trying to do. We did some surveys, not many, but really how we got there was getting our butts out of our chairs and getting into a conversation with the clinics, bouncing ideas off of them and then doing the analytics on that.

Joe: You went out there, you asked questions, you listened and then what? What were some of the major *ahas*?

President & CEO: The clients would ask, "What are you doing to make my life easier?" Oh, okay . . . so we need to think about ease of use and how we communicate that to the clinics. They'd ask, "How much money can I really make with you?" We had never been able to simply and quickly answer that question. They also asked, "How do I know that I can trust you?" We had to explain the nature of our relationship, and again, do a better job of simplifying that message. Those are the kinds of things we did.

Joe: So you figured out what the clients needed, what they wanted, and what they were looking for out of the relationship with you. And then what?

President & CEO: The reality was that we had extraordinarily low cash reserves. We had to get leaner and smarter at the same time. We had to stop spending money in areas that weren't yielding any fruit. We had to do the analytics on clinics to see which ones we needed to stop working with aggressively, and we had to be disciplined about where we were spending our cycles, whether they were technology cycles, service cycles, or out-of-resource cycles. That allowed us to figure out that we had a core set of clinics. We may work with 6,000 clinics a year, which is 25 percent of the market, ostensibly. But in reality, there are less than 1,000 that are the bread and butter of what we do.

From a resource standpoint, the reality was that we had very few resources in the field and we had clinics all over the country that needed full-out support. We started testing different models where we would do high-touch in different regions and compare it to what we would do with only remote touches in other regions. We would drop a sales rep or even an executive into an area and have them visit a bunch of clinics. We actually found that being able to have a dynamic and consistent dialogue with the clinic, finding a champion, and partnering and creating a real relationship with that champion—that was the path to getting a critical toehold and expanding our reach within those clinics. And we learned that it was much easier and more effective to do high-touch work in a clinic that was already using our service versus doing it in a clinic that had never even considered home pharmaceutical delivery. So our focus became mining the existing clinic base and not worrying about creating new clinics, unless they came to us.

Joe: You tested a couple of things, including putting an outside rep or an executive next to the clinics and visiting them. What worked and what didn't?

President & CEO: First of all, you need quality in that rep. Second of all, you need quality in the message. You've got to keep the message tight. You've got to be able to have dialogue. You don't start by saying, "This is what we do." You start by saying, "Hey, how are you doing? Where are the pressure points of your business?" Then you work to connect your value proposition to where the painpoints are.

On the question of whether or not you need an in-person or an outside resource connecting with these clinics to start the process of improvement and deeper account penetration, we've been able to do it both ways: with remote contact and with in-person contact.

The reality is that everybody has almost the same set of issues. The key is when you ask the question—what are your problems?—that you are able to link your value proposition to what their issues are. For example, some of the issues at the clinic level are that they write a lot of prescriptions and have only 30 percent compliance in a certain category, or their tech staff hates carrying food back and forth from the food shed, or the dogs that come in to board always pee on the food or open the food, or they have a lot of mice problems, or they can't keep certain drugs in stock because they're too expensive . . . or they'd really like to have a new x-ray machine, but they can't afford it because their cash is tied up with other things. Every step along the way there, you can tie back how home delivery can help alleviate that problem. On the cash issue, if you've got $25,000 in inventory, we can drop that down to $10,000, freeing up $15,000 of working capital to go out and buy that new x-ray machine that allows you to increase your service revenue.

Somebody will say, "I'm losing all these customers to 800-PetMeds." All these customers. It's unbelievable. In reality, they're probably losing one out of 20, but it's a drumbeat, they hear it all the time. They see clients walking out the door and they lose contact with those folks, and we can bring that back to them. We can increase compliance. There are all sorts of things we can do, *but we have to identify what their problems are first and then connect and link them.*

Joe: What, if anything, makes the client experience different for you being in the venture capital space?

President & CEO: First of all, it doesn't matter whether you're a publicly-traded company, a not-for-profit, or whatever. When I got here, this company was in a revenue free-fall. Employee morale was in terrible shape. The investors had zero confidence in the way the business was going. It was all those dynamics. That can hit any kind of business at any point. This isn't just about being in a venture scenario. This is about being in a challenging failure scenario that needed stabilization and fixing. You've got to start there.

When you come into these things, if you're a venture company that's going through high growth, you need a different set of resources than if you're in a venture company that's going through massively distressed times. I think it's very rare that the same person is going to have the DNA to handle both of those situations. And the reason that's important relative to this book is that one of the key attributes of leadership is to recognize when you're not the expert for a given situation. It doesn't mean that you can't be the leader, but if your expertise is operational turnarounds and not high growth, even if high growth is part of where the business is going, you have to be able to say, "You know what, I'm going to focus on the ops, the strategy, the financial side of things, and I'm going to find somebody who can do the growth piece."

That's what got us to entreQuest, which brought expertise capabilities into the picture that we didn't have off-the-shelf here. A very important part of leadership is understanding when and how to pull in what you need and have that complement what you've already got, regardless of whether you're flush with cash or not. And again, your role is to make sure that the effort has the alignment and the urgency in order to make it execute.

Joe: Once you got a firm handle on what the clients were looking for, how do you tell the story now?

President & CEO: I would say that it was less a function of having a clear handle and more a function of saying we've clarified the message, we've retrained sales staff. We've identified the rough profile of a good target audience, and now we're going to go out there and show that we can move the needle—and not just move the needle but really bend it in a big way. We recognized that given the limited resources we had, we had to have a pretty tight scope to what we were doing, and part of this was to demonstrate to the company and to the investors that we could create results.

A big part of it was also to show the sales team that they could do what they didn't think they could do before, and not only that they could do it, but that it was skilled and it helped us. In some ways, it helped us identify the right people in the sales team. It absolutely helped us dial into what we needed to do from a message standpoint. As far as achieving what we were trying to do, we had an idea. We had to use laser focus to make it work. We had to demonstrate that it was scalable; it was still part of the change process of the organization, both internally and externally.

Joe: How did you know it was working?

President & CEO: We knew it was working because we measured the impact on the clinics based on the volume of prescriptions and orders that were coming in. It would start off a little slow, but then it took off.

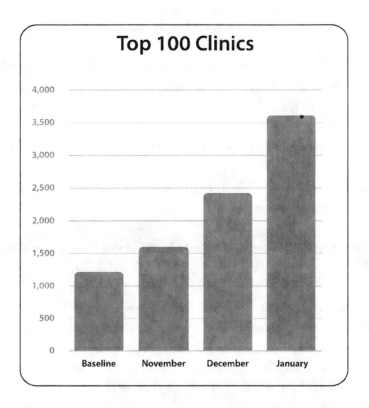

Again, the premise was to get people to be believers and they'll jump on the ship. Get them to understand what you're doing and they'll become avid users of your solution. That's what we did. We knew it was working because we could see the results. At first there was a doubling and then a tripling, and then even more prescription volume across a wide subset of clinics. For example, we targeted 150 clinics in the first ninety-day blitz. It wasn't that we were targeting our best clinics, either; we had an assortment that included low-volume up to medium-volume clinics, and we put incentives in place for the sales team based on what kind of multiples they were getting. There were no incentives at the clinic level or anything like that.

We took the sales team, which at the time was twelve or fourteen people, and set them out to really drive home the message in those 150 clinics. The first month we saw minimal results, but by the second month and thereafter, we saw an absolutely steady stream of increase across every clinic dimension.

So we saw that the message worked. Then the challenge was taking what we learned in the blitz and applying it over and over and over again into subsequent blitz efforts.

Joe: Where would the company be if you hadn't done what you did?

President & CEO: If we hadn't done what we did, the company would have bled to death years ago.

Joe: Anything you would have done differently as you went through this?

President & CEO: I would have done more, faster. I think another great attribute of a leader is being able to recognize not only what you need to do or how badly you need to get there, but also to convince others that they need to get there even sooner. Sometimes you think you don't have perfect information or even have critical mass information, but the reality is you know what you need to do. The answer is right there in front of you and you've got to make it happen.

entreQuest

DID YOU KNOW?

entreQuest helps companies realize their extraordinary potential to Grow Regardless by bettering the lives of their people, the experience of their clients, and the condition of their communities.

VISIT OUR WEBSITE
TO EXPLORE MORE:

SPEAKING

Joe Mechlinski brings his simple, yet powerful growth strategy to thousands each year giving business leaders the tools to overcome inertia and even reverse a decline by becoming a mission-driven organizations.

PRODUCTS & TRAINING

entreQuest's programs, such as Leadership Essentials, EPIC, and The eQ Sales Effect, were developed from proven growth strategies and practices to inspire CEOs, entrepreneurs, and business leaders to build mission-driven, high growth companies.

CONSULTING

entreQuest Business Consultants employ the 'Grow Regardless' approach in all their consulting engagements. With diverse expertise, entreQuest helps growing companies, large and small, to achieve remarkable results by providing high-level strategic planning, tailored growth plans, and ground-level implementation support.

www.entrequest.com | 410-276-1186

CPSIA information can be obtained at www.ICGtesting.com
Printed in the USA
LVOW062031240113

317126LV00001BA/1/P